Write Now!

Write Now!

Publishing with Young Authors

PreK—Grade 2

Karyn Wellhousen Tunks &
Rebecca McMahon Giles

HEINEMANN
Portsmouth, NH

Heinemann

A division of Reed Elsevier Inc.

361 Hanover Street

Portsmouth, NH 03801–3912

www.heinemann.com

Offices and agents throughout the world

Library of Congress Cataloging-in-Publication Data

Tunks, Karyn.

  Write now! : publishing with young authors, preK–grade 2 / Karyn Tunks, Rebecca Giles.

     p. cm.

  Includes bibliographical references.

  ISBN-13: 978-0-325-00911-7 (pbk. : alk. paper)

  ISBN-10: 0-325-00911-2

  1. Child authors. 2. Creative writing. 3. Language arts (Elementary).

  4. Children—Writing. I. Giles, Rebecca. II. Title.

  PN171.C5T86 2007

  808'.02'83—dc22   2006030209

Editor: Jim Strickland

Production: Lynne Costa

Cover design: Jenny Jensen Greenleaf

Cover photograph: Rebecca McMahon Giles

Typesetter: SPi Publisher Services

Manufacturing: Steve Bernier

Printed in the United States of America on acid-free paper

11 10 09 08 07 VP 1 2 3 4 5

To the precious children in my life: Jackson, Katy Jo, Ryan, and Coral.

—K.W.T.

To my mom—the mother I hope to be.
—R.M.G.

Contents

Acknowledgments

We wish to acknowledge the many people who played a behind-the-scenes role in the writing of this book. First, the many children whose own experiences as writers have served as an inspiration and provided us with ideas and examples used throughout this book. Specifically, we'd like to recognize the children in K5A at Mobile Christian School during the 2005–2006 school year. Thanks to these children, their accommodating parents, and the supportive school administration and faculty for the opportunity to field-test all of the ideas and strategies recommended. Next, we thank our acquisition editor, Lois Bridges, our development editor, Jim Strickland, and our production editor, Lynne Costa, as well as those who served as reviewers, for their trust and suggestions. We also acknowledge our colleagues at the University of South Alabama for their support and encouragement during this project. We especially thank our friends Paige Baggett, Nancy Gaillard, Bobbie Solley, and Lisa White for their encouragement. Finally, we want to express our appreciation to our husbands, Jeff and Bryan, for their patience and understanding while we worked on this project and to our children, Katy Jo, Jackson, Jay, and Kade, whose personal experiences are revealed throughout this book.

Introduction

When I ask students enrolled in my college classes to recall their own experiences with writing in elementary school, their memories fall into two distinct categories. First, there are those who remember learning about grammar, by painfully diagramming sentences to identify subject, verb, adverb, and other parts of speech. The second, more enthusiastic category includes students with sentimental recollections of composing a special piece of writing. These pieces were published in some final form, and typically, the student or her parents still have it.

My personal experience falls into the second category. While in the second grade, I wrote and illustrated a series of one-page stories. The subject matter was simple observations of my eight-year-old world. Each story contained very creative, invented spellings. What gave importance to this writing was the fact that my mother published it. She sandwiched the pages between two sheets of red construction paper, punched holes along the margin, and laced together the book with green yarn. On the cover, she neatly printed, "Karyn's Book of Stories." Like my students, I still have my first book, the cover now faded to a pale pinkish-orange. It survived the last forty years because of the satisfaction it brought me at the age of eight. Experiences such as these underscore the whole purpose behind publishing children's writing. Publishing gives special importance to a piece of writing, so much so that children will hold onto their published pieces through adulthood.

In this book, we have provided you the reader with the basic philosophy behind our approach to teaching young children to write—publish early and often. This approach gives children real reasons for making the effort to write. Like many teachers, we have observed countless times the joy and satisfaction children get from seeing their spoken or written words in a final form and in sharing their story with others. In order to make this event a part of children's daily experiences, rather than a rare moment, we have devised four strategies for implementing a publishing approach to teaching writing. These strategies cover a broad range of abilities and build on one another, resulting in children who are confident, prolific, and independent writers. We also address the parallel between children's oral language and early writing and give suggestions for bridging this transition. This is important to those who teach very young children but also for primary-grade teachers so they can understand where children have come from in their language and literacy development.

We encourage you, the reader, to take the philosophy, strategies, and ideas that are presented here and mold them into your own personal teaching style and classroom environment. Rather than giving you a "how-to" manual of ways to implement the publishing approach to teaching writing, we are arming you with a toolkit full of ideas and examples. We acknowledge there is more than one way to achieve the goal of making young children feel and behave like real writers, and it is our hope that you will take what you learn here and make it your own.

A Publishing Philosophy

Why and How Young Children Write

The only reward that I look forward to is the finished piece of writing in hand.
—Erskine Caldwell

1

Most moms have a vivid memory of their child's first steps. I'll never forget the moment when I turned from the kitchen sink and found thirteen-month-old Jay standing halfway between me and the place I had left him. His grin actually widened, and he erupted in giggles, realizing that he now had an audience for his stunning accomplishment. Already pleased with himself, he became even more delighted at having his new feat witnessed. Young children feel a sense of success and awe as parents react to each developmental milestone, whether it's taking their first steps, uttering their first words, or tying their shoes by themselves for the first time.

Parents intrinsically realize the need for very young children to successfully experience the outcome of a new challenge. So, they help children experience this initial success before the child is personally motivated to exert the effort to achieve it without assistance. This is why, when the slightest interest in walking is demonstrated, countless, backbreaking hours are spent holding an infant's upstretched arms in order to lift and propel one foot in front of the other. The combination of watching others and walking with assistance informs infants about walking—what it is, how it feels, and how it works. Finally, the parents' obvious delight when those first steps are taken conveys the joy and satisfaction this act brings to others. Once these infants learn what it is to "walk," they are more willing to put forth the effort and energy required to walk unassisted. This knowledge, along with the continued smiles, kisses, and praise from significant others, is what motivates infants to walk independently.

Learning to write, like learning to walk, first requires that children experience writing, that they know what it means to write. Preschoolers are well aware of the meaning *they* attach to their squiggles and can fluently "read" a page of their own marks. But, the feeling that comes from writing words that can be read by others brings its own distinctive form of satisfaction. The International Reading Association and the National Association for the Education of Young Children have adopted a joint position statement describing developmentally appropriate practices for young children in preschool through third grade learning to read and write. This statement, which can be accessed at www.naeyc.org/about/positions/PSREAD0.asp, recognizes that children's emerging literacy skills evolve over time with practice. During this critical time period for literacy acquisition, children need print in their environment, tools to write with, adult writing models, time and encouragement to attempt writing on their own, and positive feedback from others.

Because children learn to write by writing, they need many opportunities to write daily. Although they receive a certain amount of self-satisfaction in their ability to write, it is the positive reaction of others to their writing that provides incentive for them to continue. The turning point for most famous authors was the first time they were published. According to Lucy Calkins, founding director of the Teachers College Writing Project, "Publishing matters, and it matters because it inducts us [writers] into the writerly life" (1994, p. 266). Public affirmation, and the gratifying feeling it produces, serves as the motivation for emergent writers to publish early and often. Eventually, this recognition provides incentive to carry young children through the entire writing process.

■ Publishing Defined

It is the act of publishing itself that makes writing a primary means of communication. For young children with limited attention spans, the immediate recognition and gratification that comes from publishing are the catalysts for further writing. It is others' response that affirms children's abilities as writers and, as a result, provides the motivation to continue. Our understanding of how children learn and develop has led us to broadly define publishing. The word *publish* as it is used throughout this book means "making what is known by the author available to others through writing." This definition uses the word *writing* to refer to any means of written communication, including dictation taken by an adult as well as drawing and other early forms of writing. This definition recognizes the fact that an author's willingness to share his writing is enough to consider it published. It should be noted that this broad description of publishing is not limited to work that has gone through the writing process but also includes "one-step" publishing or writing that is made available in its original form (often referred to as "first draft"). We have expanded the traditionally accepted definition of publishing to benefit emergent writers; this includes young children, children with special needs, and English language learners.

The following examples from a first-grade classroom illustrate this approach to publishing. After thoroughly examining a collection of rocks in the discovery center, Brittany writes, "sum are ruff" on the observation chart posted nearby. By recording her observation in a place where it could be read by her teacher and peers, Brittany participated in the act of publishing. The child who posts a "do not tuch" sign on a block structure in progress or notes "shhhhhh!" on a sign in the listening center has also published.

This type of publishing is designed for emerging writers, who lack the knowledge and skills necessary to sustain themselves through a multistep process in order to publish in the traditional sense. One-step publishing rewards

Family members are a popular publishing topic for young children.

children's readiness to publish even if a product has not been revised and edited. Children with special needs and English language learners also benefit from this type of publishing experience. Like all young children, they are building basic concepts of print as they begin to engage in and experiment with writing. Our perspective on publishing proposes that concepts and strategies children need to become successful writers can be acquired prior to fully assimilating all print-related knowledge. Letter recognition, sound-symbol knowledge, and fine motor skills, although necessary tools for writing proficiently, have little to do with the self-expression writing allows. These skills are more meaningful and best taught when children are actually writing within authentic contexts. This philosophy is based on the understanding that writing development occurs through genuine experiences in writing as authors receive motivational recognition and constructive feedback through sharing published works.

■ A Constructivist View of Learning

A perspective known as constructivism, which stems from the work of Piaget (1983) and Vygotsky (1962/1986), is highly favored by modern educators to explain how children learn. Constructivists maintain that children gradually construct inner cognitive structures that help them make sense of their physical and social worlds through interactions with individuals and the environment.

As children engage in the act of writing, they constantly reconstruct their understanding of written communication at higher developmental levels. As stated earlier, for young children writing involves any form of written communication, such as drawing, adult dictation, or any manner of child-produced text. Using each of these forms of writing allows children to revise and refine their ideas about concepts of print as they make and test hypotheses. This trial-and-error process of writing development begins with scribbling and depends upon feedback from more proficient writers in order to evolve.

■ Strategies for Teaching Writing

Having accepted the philosophical stance that publishing is essential to encouraging and enabling emerging writers, we have developed an approach that emphasizes repeated and varied classroom publishing opportunities. This approach utilizes four publishing strategies—dictating oral anecdotes, translating kid writing, creating cooperative chronicles, and encouraging independent authors. These strategies emphasize the benefit of publishing, individually and collaboratively, in order for emergent learners to see themselves as competent writers. Additionally, these strategies are designed to increase the likelihood of success by providing a supportive, constructive means for emerging writers to become accomplished authors.

Dictating Oral Anecdotes

Initially, young children have no early interest in the process of writing or in understanding what other authors do when they write. Instead, their primary objective is to simply share their story. In the beginning, it is of no consequence to the child that the story be recorded in any type of permanent format. Typically they are oblivious to the idea that their stories can be recorded and enjoyed again and again. They simply want to "get the story out."

Think about how you feel when something funny, exciting, or frightening happens to you. Our first reaction is to share the experience by telling a friend or family member. The same is true for young children. It is our job to show them that their stories can be preserved through writing. We want to help children understand that their oral anecdotes have value and are worthy of being recorded as stories. Emerging writers, who do not possess the skills required to write stories using conventional print, benefit from telling a story orally to an adult scribe, who takes dictation. Teachers may informally jot down stories children tell during class sharing time or casually offer to write down the child's description of a creation, such as a modeling clay animal, during learning centers. As the teacher reads the child's words back to him, he begins to recognize the power of the recorded story and the purpose of putting words on paper. Viewing his oral anecdotes in a permanent, published format is a richly rewarding experience.

Translating Kid Writing

As children become aware of the purpose and function of writing, they attempt to replicate what they observe others doing when they write. These early attempts at writing are called *kid writing* and typically include drawings, scribbles, and other markings that may be unreadable to others. In order to show children their message is important, adults listen and record children's writing as they "read" it aloud. When their efforts are recognized, children continue playing with print and eventually begin using more sophisticated forms of kid writing, which include invented spellings in which they record the sounds they hear in words. This process marks an important transition into

Hunter publishes on the dry-erase board.

writing that can be read by others. Publishing children's writing to celebrate each accomplishment serves as a strong motivator for strengthening their desire to write independently.

Creating Cooperative Chronicles

After children have had numerous opportunities to publish dictated anecdotes, teachers can introduce the concept of cooperative chronicles. This process takes different forms as children write interactively within a group, moving the child to a less egocentric view. The teacher guides the composition of the group's story through scaffolding by posing questions, asking for clarification, and making suggestions. Using this process, the teacher is challenging children to clarify misunderstandings, expand ideas, interpret meaning, and respond to the text as they revise their original drafts. Cooperative chronicles also can include discussions between a teacher and an individual child about her ideas, topics, or drawings. While dictated anecdotes and kid writing are accepted at face value to build children's success as published writers, cooperative chronicles introduce the process of revising and editing prior to publishing.

Encouraging Independent Authors

After many successes as published authors, children develop an interest in writing that is strong enough to sustain them through the entire writing process. With each success, they become more devoted to writing rich, inviting pieces that will entertain and inform their audience. The final step to becoming an accomplished author is to complete all stages of the writing process independently.

By the time children have reached the point that they can create an independent product, they understand the joy that comes from publishing and sharing stories with others. Through working within a group, they have learned what kinds of questions to ask and recognize when clarification may be needed. By examining writing at different points of revision, they have witnessed first-hand the importance of editing.

Accomplished authors have learned to differentiate between good and excellent writing from other readers' reactions to their published work and their own feelings about favorite pieces. Another lesson that has been learned is the realization that a considerable amount of work and effort goes into publishing an exemplary piece of writing. Because the children fully understand the task of taking a piece from prewriting through editing before finally publishing, they no longer want to dedicate time and energy to every topic that pops into their head but begin to choose selectively what they will publish.

■ Publishing First

Young children, and new authors of any age, are primarily interested in writing as a means of sharing their ideas. The process required of good writers is a long and arduous one. Beginning writers do not possess the patience or attention necessary to complete the process from prewriting to publication. In order to sustain their interest in writing, young children need to see their work in a published form early and often.

Abundant early publishing in a supportive literacy environment firmly embeds the idea that young children themselves are authors, filled with stories and information worthy of being committed to paper for the purpose of enjoying at a later date or sharing with those not initially present. This novel approach to teaching writing—publishing first—is an engaging and motivational means of introducing emerging literacy learners into the world of writing.

2 Supporting Oral Language

Talking Their Way to Publishing

Words are, of course, the most powerful drug used by mankind.

—Rudyard Kipling

I'd love to say that my son's first word was "Momma," but I'd be lying. I am, however, slightly consoled by the fact that it wasn't "Daddy" either. It was "ball," followed shortly thereafter by his first sentence—"Kade play ball." Kade's early language accurately reflected his favorite pastime—rolling, throwing, kicking, bouncing, carrying, or just playing with balls of any and every kind. Language, whether oral or written, reflects an individual's unique self, likes, dislikes, and greatest loves. It is his voice. Providing opportunities to communicate and experiences to communicate about gives children the means to first discover and then share themselves with others.

■ Learning Language

Learning language, both oral and written, is an active process in which children acquire the ability to use language correctly through a process of making and learning from their mistakes. For example, "I eated ice cream" is replaced with "I ate ice cream" as a preschooler's knowledge of and experience with past tense verbs increases. Similarly, children's writing follows this same trial-and-error process. Figure 2–1 compares the acquisition of oral and written language.

Figure 2–1 *Acquiring language*

	Oral	**Written**
Initial attempts	babbling	scribbling
Early attempts	word approximations	letter strings
First communication	single word utterances (a.k.a. holophrastic speech)	initial consonants
Increased clarity	two words combined (a.k.a. telegraphic speech)	phonetic spelling environmental printing
Further refined	simple sentences inflection	advanced phonetic spelling conventional spelling of high-frequency/sight words appropriate spacing left-right—return sweep some capitalization uses period correctly
Standard—Adult	grammatically correct rich vocabulary conversational turn-taking	grammatically correct rich vocabulary correct capitalization correct punctuation

Learning to Talk

Oral language develops rapidly from birth through age three. A major milestone in a child's language development occurs the first time he says an understandable word. First words typically appear at between nine and fifteen months. These words, or word approximations, appear in the form of names for significant people and objects in the child's life, such as "ba ba" for bottle, and are used to have basic needs met. This holophrastic speech, the use of a single word to communicate an entire thought or idea, continues until about eighteen to twenty-four months. At this point, a child begins putting words, usually nouns and verbs, together. This telegraphic speech is limited but powerful in its ability to communicate a message—"me go" or "want juice." Longer utterances and complete sentences appear between three and five years of age.

By age four, children have a rich vocabulary in which they understand and use thousands of words. By the time they enter school at five or six, children have acquired most of the elements of adult language and possess an oral vocabulary between 5,000 and 10,000 words, depending upon both biological and environmental influences. Although children have mastered most grammatical rules, they continue to refine and expand their speech throughout the elementary grades, learning as many as twenty new words a day (Berk 2002).

Learning to Speak a Second Language

For second-language learners, a strong foundation in their first language promotes school achievement in a second language (Cummins 1979). Thus, young English language learners are more likely to become readers and writers of English when they are already familiar with the vocabulary and concepts in their primary language. For this reason, language experiences should be regarded as an additive process, allowing children to maintain their home language while also learning to speak and read English (Wong Fillmore 1991). Introducing non-English materials and resources helps support and validate children's first language while they acquire oral proficiency in English. When teachers simultaneously support English acquisition and the child's home language and culture, the child can become bilingual and biliterate (Morrow 2005a, p. 13).

Learning to Write

Writing, as an expressive mode of language, is closely linked to oral language and is learned in much the same way. Since oral and written language share common vocabulary and grammar, it is not necessary for a child who already knows how to talk to learn an entirely new system of communication in order to learn to write. Learning to write, however, is more difficult than learning to talk since it adds the need for understanding symbol knowledge to the understanding of sound and meaning required when speaking (Roskos, Christie, and Rigels 2003).

Scribbling is the beginning point for expressing thoughts and ideas in both drawing and writing. In both, scribbling represents children's fascination with the process of producing marks as they actively explore and manipulate the medium. Through repeated experiences with scribbling, children begin to recognize the difference between drawing and writing. It is at this point that two different kinds of scribbles are used. Writing scribbles that take on a distinctly printlike form, appear in lines across the page. However, individual writing scribbles vary greatly, and their similarity to print may not always be easily identifiable. The child's intention to draw or write may be revealed only within the context in which the marks are made, as opposed to viewing the finished product. For example, a child's attempt to make a shopping list may be recognized as such only when the child is actually observed creating the list while playing grocery store. The true distinction between drawing and writing scribbles occurs as the child, realizing that writing is something that can be read, "reads" his own scribbled writing—"milk, bread, and chocolate-chip cookies."

The awareness that a world of pictures exists separately from a world of print is a major discovery for the emerging writer (Schickedanz and Casbergue 2004). A child's understanding of this distinction is revealed when she moves from pointing to and naming objects in an illustration (that is, "dog" or "boy") to running her finger across the text and saying "once upon a time there was a boy with a dog . . . ." Her understanding is also revealed when her attempts to write no longer look like the things she is writing about (pictures) but resemble print more closely.

■ Environment as an Influence on Learning Language

Although language learning is innate to children (Chomsky 1965), seven environmental conditions must be in place for language learning to occur—immersion, demonstration, expectation, responsibility, use, approximation, and response—each serving a necessary purpose (Cambourne 1987). When combined, these conditions lead to effective language learning and facilitate children's progress as they learn to communicate by talking and writing.

From birth children are *immersed* in a world full of language. They routinely hear conversations among family members and friends, are privy to caregiver's informative commentaries as they complete routine tasks, and listen to commercial language production, such as radio announcements and television broadcasts. All of these experiences provide opportunities for children to hear language in various forms and contexts. Similarly, children's knowledge of written language begins long before they enter school as they encounter print in their environment. Infants are exposed to print from day one, with an "I'm a Big Brother" t-shirt or a framed birth announcement adorning the nursery wall. Such encounters continue for preschoolers when they open birthday cards, observe Mom copy a recipe, or write a letter to Santa Claus. It is through these natural encounters with print that children's awareness of the value and usefulness of writing increases.

Children witness how language works each time they hear or see it used. Adult models provide information about the types and purposes of language when they communicate, either orally or in writing, in the presence of children. Parents *demonstrate* the purpose of speaking each time they are heard having a conversation. In the same way, they demonstrate the purpose of writing each time their children see them taking a phone message, writing a check, or sending an email.

Infants learning to speak their native tongue is an amazing feat; yet, it is readily accepted that every child, barring a severe disability, will learn to talk. This universal assumption that children can and will succeed in learning to talk is communicated to children through adults' words and actions. We have an *expectation* that children will talk, which contributes to young children's success as they learn oral language. This same level of expectation is equally necessary for success when children are learning to write. Because children often view themselves through the eyes of others, it essential that significant adult influences view children as writers if they are going to come to view themselves as writers as well.

Children are ultimately *responsible* for their own language learning. Each child's pace and order for acquiring language is determined by his personal experiences. Whether speaking or writing, the child must be empowered to make decisions regarding what is communicated, to whom, and when, in order for true learning to result. Children must be allowed to construct their own understanding of language actively through a process of problem solving. Merely imitating adults or rote learning does not afford necessary opportunities for children to figure out independently how language works.

Children internalize the conventions of language as they *use* language for meaningful and functional purposes. It is by using language that children have the opportunity to apply recently acquired knowledge (of word order, vocabulary, or plurals) and practice skills (verbal expression, intonation, or conversational turn-taking). New knowledge is clarified and skills are refined when sufficient time and opportunity are provided to develop them fully. Thus, children benefit from frequent opportunities to engage in conversation as well as many, varied opportunities to write for real and relevant purposes.

As children apply their newfound language abilities, perfection is neither expected nor required. In fact, close *approximations* to conventional speech and writing are not only expected but accepted as a necessary part of learning. As children attempt to incorporate new vocabulary or use verb tenses, they often make mistakes. These mistakes, such as saying "catched" or "runned," result in their learning through trial and error. This allows a child to first make a mistake before she can learn from it. Adults should readily accept a child's production of letterlike scribbles with the same level of enthusiasm and encouragement with which his babbling is met. Early attempts at writing should not only be accepted but also valued as a necessary step in learning to write proficiently.

Adults' *responses* to children's language use allow the children to clarify misconceptions and self-correct mistakes. For example, a toddler might say, "I saw two mans walking," to which Dad might reply, "Oh, you saw two men walking," causing the child to reconsider his addition of "s" to "man" as an indication of more than one. Likewise, providing the written response "I love you, too" to a child's written declaration of "i luv u" causes the child to reevaluate his original message. In both examples, feedback was supplied naturally and without judgment through an expected response. When a constructive, nonthreatening response is given, this feedback provides the means by which children continually refine and improve their use of language.

■ Learning Language in the Classroom

Language is a necessary ingredient for learning in general and an essential part of literacy learning. While experience needs language to give it form, language needs experience to give it meaning. Children must have something to talk about. A child who has a storehouse of words learned through authentic play and life experiences brings a valuable asset to each new encounter. Therefore, young children's oral language development must be strengthened and reinforced in the classroom.

The home culture of children plays a powerful role in shaping their oral language. Teachers must learn about the culture of the children they teach to increase their understanding of how experiences outside of school shape the perspective of children and their families. Teachers should also recognize that children learn to function in multiple contexts easily and understand how this applies to language and literacy learning. Standard English must be modeled for children whose primary language is not English as well as for those who speak nonstandard forms of the English language. Children's language of origin should be respected and sensitivity used as Standard English is introduced and reinforced.

Young children need numerous opportunities to practice oral language skills. Children learn language best by using it daily in authentic, spontaneous episodes. Conversation between friends, for example, occurs without adult assistance, and as a result, it is extremely stimulating for children. The classroom that encourages talking provides a necessary ingredient for learning simply by giving children the opportunity to use oral language in meaningful ways. The optimal situation is one in which children spend the majority of their school day communicating with one another as well as with adults. This is best achieved in a classroom that is organized into learning centers where children are able to discuss, debate, and converse with their peers about topics that arise out of their play. (Chapter 3 will provide more information on learning centers.)

As teachers, we also need to plan and prepare activities that promote language development and build confidence in children's abilities to communicate orally. Effective questioning, book talks, show-and-tell, role play, choral speaking, Readers' Theater, story retelling, storytelling, dramatizations, and puppet shows should be staples in the early childhood classroom. All of these activities, and many others, promote children's use of oral language while enriching their general knowledge of language.

■ Questioning Techniques

Knowing when and how to ask an appropriate question is a highly desirable skill. In addition to promoting children's oral language, questioning is a valuable teaching and assessment tool. The most widely used taxonomy for framing questions is the one developed by Bloom (1969), which identifies six levels of thinking in hierarchical order from simple (knowledge) to complex (evaluation). Figure 2–2 illustrates the application of Bloom's taxonomy to the well-known children's classic, *The Very Hungry Caterpillar* by Eric Carle, with an example question for each level.

Involving English language learners (ELLs) in content-specific classroom discussions can be highly successful if teachers develop appropriate strategies

---

Figure 2–2 *Using Bloom's Taxonomy with* The Very Hungry Caterpillar

Level of Thinking	Sample Questions

Knowledge
    identification and recall
    of information
	What did the little caterpillar eat?

Comprehension
    organization and
    selection of facts/ideas
	What happened to the caterpillar at the end
	    of this story?

Application
    use of information
	Why is the amount of food that the
	    caterpillar ate important?

Analysis
    compare and contrast
	How do the foods eaten Monday through
	    Friday compare to those the caterpillar
	    ate on Saturday?

Synthesis
    combining ideas to form
    new whole
	How could the caterpillar have
	    avoided a stomachache?

Evaluation
    develop opinion or
    make a judgment
	What do you think about the caterpillar's
	    food choices?

---

for including all learners. Teachers should choose easy questions for their ELLs, structure the form of the question to their current language ability, and accept single words or short phrases as correct answers rather than insisting that ELLs speak in full sentences. Providing ELLs with advance notice of the questions they will be responsible for answering allows time for them to think and prepare their answers adequately.

■ Read Alouds

The positive impact of reading aloud on children's reading development is well documented (Trelease 2006); it provides numerous benefits for children's oral language development as well. Reading aloud builds children's vocabulary, provides opportunities for children to express their feelings, and exposes them to various language forms and dialects. The language of books introduces children to a wealth of words not readily encountered in their everyday lives.

Reading aloud provides motivation and models for publishing.

Children internalize the rich vocabulary present in children's literature through repeated exposure. For example, Maurice Sendak's wild things gnash their terrible teeth, and Papa's echo comes threading through the trees in *Owl Moon* (Yolen and Schoenherr 1987). Cultural, geographical, and historical considerations influence an author's word choice as he attempts to obtain clarity while maintaining authenticity. As a result, children hear a wide range of words in books that they would not hear anywhere else. Further, the context of the story, possibly coupled with class discussion, allows children to assign meaning to new words heard.

Reading aloud also provides opportunities for children to build empathy and explore their feelings. Children's literature provides a practical avenue for addressing difficult issues, such as divorce and death. Wrapped in the security of fictional characters and faraway places, children feel free to express personal views and controversial opinions of cultural expectations and socially acceptable behaviors regarding prejudices and stereotypes.

Reading aloud exposes children to various forms of language and dialects. Hearing, discussing, and dramatizing published stories aids children in adopting Standard English for personal use and is preferable to constant verbal correction by adults, often interpreted as judgmental and critical. Children are also exposed to regional and cultural dialects through literature. Appalachian dialect appears in *When I was Young in the Mountains* (Rylant 1993), while Black English vernacular is employed in *Sweet Clara and the Freedom Quilt* (Hopkinson 1995). In addition to colloquial speech, books such as *Jambo Means Hello: Swahili Alphabet Book* (Feelings and Feelings 1992) and *Abuela* (Dorros and Kleven 1997) incorporate words and phrases from languages other than English into the text.

■ Role-playing

Re-enacting familiar stories promotes emergent literacy through children's active participation in role-playing (Soundy 1993). When children act out a story, they are extending the performance to include themselves (Sipe 2002). Pellegrini and Galda (1982) found that the active involvement and social interaction involved in role-playing significantly improves children's comprehension of a story and increases their story-retelling ability. Although props and costumes may enhance children's performance, neither is necessary for beneficial role-playing experiences within the classroom. Spontaneous performances are possible with the use of "narration improvisation" in which the teacher acts as narrator, telling the story with needed pauses for actors to perform actions and/or provide dialogue (Sierra 1991).

As children become more proficient at reading, Readers' Theater takes precedence over role-playing. In Readers' Theater, each child assumes a role and reads the character's lines from the scripts. Readers' Theater provides a legitimate reason and meaningful context for rereading text, which is known to increase comprehension, fluency, and expression. Martinez, Roser, and Strecker (1999) found that second-graders who regularly participated in Readers' Theater gained, on average, more than a year's growth in reading. Further, Readers' Theater promotes cooperative interaction and increases reading appeal. In addition to boosting listening and speaking skills, Readers' Theater performances can enhance general self-confidence while improving a child's perception of himself as a reader. The security of having a script present combined with the relaxed, comfortable format provides the most shy child or reluctant reader with a sense of security. The Internet is an invaluable source for locating scripts. Scripts of popular tales can be found on the Internet, such as Aaron Shepard's Page (www.aaronshep.com/rt/) or www.readerstheater.net, which offers new scripts the first of each month.

Although not necessary, name tags hung around each child's neck can identify the characters. A script may be performed for several days, put away, then reintroduced later in the school year. Name tags and copies of scripts can be placed in large, re-sealable food storage bags or envelopes for quick access at a later time. This form of drama offers a maximum return on a minimal investment because it does not require extensive preparation, fancy costumes, extravagant props, or even a stage. Best of all, Readers' Theater requires no memorization on the part of the performers, making "instant" readings possible. By following the steps in Figure 2–3, a teacher can involve children in a meaningful reading activity immediately.

Retelling Stories

Retelling involves asking children to do simply what the name implies—summarize a story or selection that they have heard or read. The retelling can occur in oral or written form. The value of children's involvement in verbally reconstructing storybook events in individual or cooperative settings has been shown by several studies. Morrow (1985, 1986) found that story retelling increased children's oral language and comprehension skills while developing their sense of story structure. Story retelling activates a cognitive organization consistent with story schema (Merritt and Liles 1989). A child must first conceptualize the story—including characters, setting, and plot—in order to retell it effectively; thus, the use of these structural elements improves with practice in retelling.

Figure 2–3 *Readers' Theater in six simple steps*

Step 1: **Select, adapt, duplicate, and distribute scripts.**
Scripts for young children should be limited to two to three pages.

Step 2: **Read the script aloud.**
Hearing the script read aloud affords the luxury of having correct pronunciation, appropriate expression, and accurate inflection modeled.

Step 3: **Assign parts.**
Parts are given to individuals, pairs, or small groups of children. The first time a script is used, each participant will need to spend a few minutes underlining or highlighting their assigned lines in the script.

Step 4: **Rehearse the script.**
Readers practice reading parts independent of other performers.

Step 5: **Assemble the readers.**
There is no right way to arrange participants for Readers' Theater. Assembling readers for performances can entail gathering on a carpet area, placing chairs in a circle, or standing readers in front of the room. When seated, children can stand as they read. When standing, a podium provides a special touch.

Step 6: **Perform the script.**
The script is read aloud for an audience of classmates, parents, or younger peers.

As children gain experience in retelling stories, they can determine what should be included in what order, resulting in less fractured and more sequentially correct accounts (De Temple and Tabors 1996), while expanding vocabulary and increasing oral expression. Story retelling provides practice in narration, allows children to differentiate between formal book language and informal conversation (Soundy 1993), promotes positive attitudes toward stories and books, and builds interest in learning to read. Morrow (1986) found an additional benefit of frequent retelling to be an increase in the oral language complexity of kindergarteners when dictating their original stories. Because children learn through imitation, retelling stories is not only enjoyable but also a valuable activity for any age.

As a means of assessment, retelling has the potential for supplying more information about a child's understanding than having the child respond to questions, which may influence responses or provide unintentional cues. Retellings also provide the opportunity to move beyond literal comprehension as they show what has been implied or inferred in addition to what has been merely grasped (Irwin and Mitchell 1983). Furthermore, retelling demonstrates a child's ability to construct text, provides insight into the thought processes, and provides a venue for assessing the quality of language used (Gunning 2004).

■ Storytelling

Storytelling strongly attracts children to books (Ritchie, James-Szanton, and Howes 2003) and motivates children to read and write themselves (Roney 1989). Considered the oldest art form, storytelling can be used to encourage children to create, tell, write, and read stories of their own. Stories from traditional oral literature are recommended for beginning storytellers, particularly fables, which are short, quick, and easy to remember. *Fables* by Arnold Lobel (1983) offers original tales filled with animal characters sharing basic morals as an alternative to traditional fable favorites. When teachers close the book and simply tell familiar stories, they are assisting children in developing imagination and thinking creatively. The storytelling audience must be active participants in order to successfully visualize the scenes and characters being described. Creating such mental imagery enhances both literal and inferential comprehension (Nelson 1989). As children listen to their teachers tell stories, they also learn how to tell stories. Storytelling provides a powerful and enjoyable language experience for young children and is often supported by simple props.

Literature Props

Literature props assist children in constructing and expressing their understanding of stories by providing concrete visual aids for accurately recalling detailed, chronological events. In addition to increasing oral language opportunities, furnishing simple props instills motivation, sparks imaginations, and launches children on an adventure of retelling, rereading, and writing. Early childhood educators have been utilizing an array of props, such as picture cards and flannel-board pieces, to enhance group storybook reading for a number of years; however, these devices were primarily used in whole-group, teacher-directed activities. As the focus in literacy instruction is moving away from such strategies to those that promote children's own search for meaning, the same props are being used in more independent, self-generated activities for the purpose of encouraging children's oral retellings (Soundy 1993). Brown (1977) suggests that children's story comprehension improves when they mentally reconstruct the events and arrange pictures of the story in sequential order since this requires building an internal representation of the story.

The inclusion of props during retelling provides children with additional support and assists them in getting started, including details, and concluding stories. Soundy and Gallagher (1993) found that using story props resulted in an increased number of words in the retellings of four- and five-year-old children. Though children's comprehension improves with frequent practice in retelling, understanding is further facilitated through the active reconstruction of events, similar to that of role-playing, which occurs when physically manipulating tangible objects.

Children's manipulation of props while retelling a story assists in their mental recreation of events. The key is to keep children participating actively throughout the retelling experience. This is usually most effective when retellings are initiated individually or in a small group. Limiting the number of children participating allows increased opportunities for every child to interact with the props. Having two or more children retell a story jointly is especially helpful when a large amount of dialogue is used. A few minutes should be allowed for playful investi-

Maggie Rose uses a sock puppet to retell The Very Hungry Caterpillar.

gation whenever new props are introduced. This break will reduce the possibility of children being distracted from the retelling by the props' interesting features.

Familiar stories with uncomplicated plots and a limited number of characters and events are a good choice for retellings by young children. Predictable books, which have a highly structured pattern, are another viable option. Those that contain a repetitive phrase, such as *The Gingerbread Man* (Ayelsworth and McClintock 1998) or a repetitive plot, like *If You Give a Mouse a Cookie* (Numeroff and Bond 1985), enable children to anticipate what happens next. In addition to these literary characteristics, the stories selected should elicit an enthusiastic response from the children, who will be doing the retelling. The number of props used varies, but it tends to increase with children's age and experience.

■ Publishing Language

Whether oral or written, language is about sharing. Both speaking and writing are means of communication that provide a vehicle for self-expression. Everything children learn about language while speaking benefits them as writers, just as all knowledge of language learned through writing improves their oral abilities. Children's sole reason to write is that they have something to share, which makes writing without publishing pointless.

3 | Providing a Writing Environment

Setting the Stage for Publishing

By writing much, one learns to write well.
—Robert Southey

Many young women visualize each detail of their wedding day. But, I began planning my child's nursery before I was pregnant or even yet married. I knew that regardless of whether my firstborn was a boy or girl, the child would come home to a room of classic storybook characters. When the time finally arrived, life-size figures were painted carefully on every wall, shelves were stocked with a rich assortment of books, and a mobile of familiar characters—Franklin, Clifford, Pooh, and Curious George—dangled over the crib. I loved this room! And, it was with a sense of sadness that years later I applied the coats of primer to make way for a "big boy" room.

It's obvious to all who know him that my son shares my love of stories and books. Whether this was inherited or grew from his early exposure, no one knows. We do know that a child's surroundings play a substantial role in his growth and learning, particularly in the area of language and literacy acquisition. Like learning to talk, children's conceptual understanding of writing begins naturally through exposure to printed language in the environment. Thus, the significant influence of the classroom environment, both physical and affective, should be given special attention to ensure that children's writing development is well supported. Creating a stimulating and interactive classroom containing purposeful opportunities to communicate using oral and written language helps children build positive attitudes toward writing and about themselves as writers.

■ An Effective Arrangement

An optimum classroom design presents publishing as an integral part of the curriculum, as children voluntarily use writing to communicate with adults and classmates in various ways throughout the day. In an ideal writing environment, the arrangement, equipment, supplies, and displays come together to encourage children's interaction with print-related materials. These encounters promote children's knowledge of print concepts and prompt publishing in contexts that emulate real-life situations.

Any classroom, regardless of size and furnishings, can become an effective writing environment by using learning centers, "multipurpose areas within a classroom where equipment and materials are organized to promote active, child-centered learning" (Kieff and Casbergue 2000, p. 66). Although learning happens throughout the classroom, the term *learning centers* describes an arrangement where specific places in the classroom are organized and supplied to facilitate learning in small groups. Learning centers provide a systematic method to manage space, materials, and time and a way to meet the individual needs of children while giving them responsibility for their own learning. Typical learning center activities, such as using a magnifying glass, pounding clay, listening to stories, creating a collage, putting together puzzles, scooping sand, building with blocks, and role-playing all reinforce the development of auditory, visual, and tactile experiences needed to interact with books and print (Gentile and Hoot 1983).

Teachers who value writing provide print-related materials that promote writing. Writing during centers allows children to imitate the writing behaviors that they have observed in the course of everyday events. In contrast, workbooks, worksheets, and color pages, which do not provide authentic writing experiences, present little opportunity for children to imitate the real writers (parents, siblings, and teachers) they observe in the world around them.

Integrating writing materials in different areas of the classroom allows children to playfully practice writing free from pressure and unrealistic or predetermined expectations. Strickland and Morrow (1989) reported that more literacy behaviors took place in play areas equipped with thematically chosen literacy materials than in rooms without such materials.

Vukelich and Valentine (1990) discovered that adding literacy props to the play areas in a kindergarten classroom greatly increased the amount of time children engaged in literate behaviors during play periods. Similarly, Vukelich (1990) reported more writing behavior when paper, pencils, note pads, books, magazines, signs, stationery, and other print-rich props were included in the dramatic play center. In much the same way, Neuman and Roskos (1990) found that creating specific play scenes with corresponding literacy props allowed children to make greater use of reading and writing within their play. Children's reading and writing became more purposeful in literacy-enriched play environments, and these behaviors bound the play into a coherent theme.

Preschoolers learn about language through play, using their play experiences as topics of conversations and stories (Morrison and Rusher 1999). Similarly, school-age children's time in learning centers provides a context for their conversations and experiences to write about. Center activities provide relevant and meaningful experiences to be used as topics of conversations and stories while also providing the context for publishing.

Using Learning Centers

Learning centers take optimum advantage of young children's natural abilities, interests, and enthusiasm for learning while meeting the individual needs of diverse learners. Young children learn almost exclusively by moving, playing, and doing. They construct knowledge actively by exploring the world around them during socially meaningful interactions. Teachers, therefore, can best facilitate learning by providing organized centers that offer hands-on opportunities for discovery learning by individuals or small groups. Learning centers can be offered in all content areas, on a variety of levels, and they enhance development across all domains—social, emotional, physical, and cognitive. Learning centers allow children to apply skills and concepts introduced through direct instruction and use related vocabulary, while providing opportunity for in-depth study. Further, learning centers enable early-childhood teachers to work with individuals or small groups while other children are actively engaged in a variety of self-selected activities.

Learning centers that provide opportunity for pretend play are particularly important to children's literacy development. Pretending an object has a different meaning or use other than that for which it was intended is an important step in mastering the concept of symbolic representation that is necessary for reading and writing (Vygotsky 1967). According to Piaget (1962), symbolic play occurs when children mentally allow one object to represent another. For example, a child holds a block to her ear and has a one-sided, pretend conversation with her grandmother. In this situation, the block has become a symbol for a telephone. "These symbolic activities rely on children's abilities to create meaning in their minds and to express that meaning through gesture, language, intonation and objects" (Nourot and Van Hoorn 1991, p. 41). Because the written symbols of language depend on the reader's ability to perform symbolic transfers, symbolic play is a developmental precursor to reading and writing (Roskos et al. 1995). All three activities—symbolic play, reading, and writing—require the ability to use words, gestures, or mental images to stand for actual objects, events, or actions.

The inclusion of costumes, props, and puppets in learning centers provides opportunities for language and literacy development through symbolic play. In first- and second-grade classrooms, the emphasis moves from dramatic play to drama. How children use props is limited only by the children's own imaginations. This is also true of print-related props. A note pad and pencil can elicit behaviors that range from taking food orders and making appointments to writing a script and creating cue cards for class productions.

By observing children's play in centers, teachers can determine the best way to use learning centers. Periodically rotating certain centers sustains children's interest and is a good use of limited space. Teachers may choose to track children's preferences by keeping a tally of the centers children visit using the checklist provided (See Appendix A). This information can be used to encourage children to try centers they do not typically choose.

Center Materials

Materials for each center should span a wide range of possibilities, selected for their capacity to be used by children of varying ages and abilities to meet multiple instructional purposes. Before being used independently, teachers can introduce materials and demonstrate how to use them. As with the centers themselves, materials should be rotated periodically to maintain interest and, perhaps, coordinate with the current theme of study.

Developing Print Concepts

Print concepts are easily promoted in meaningful ways by stocking learning centers with materials that encourage reading and writing. Teachers can be creative in providing these materials but should make selections based on an item's appropriateness, authenticity, and functionality (Neuman and Roskos 1990). *Appropriate* materials are those chosen with a particular age and stage of development in mind, such as bright watercolor markers and unlined paper for preschool children. *Authenticity* is achieved when the materials are typical of what might be found in a similar adult setting. For example, pencils and drafting paper can be found in an architect's office and can also be used by children planning a construction in art or blocks. *Functional* materials are those that are practical and useful for children and the learning center where the materials are located. For instance, data charts, observation logs, and graphs are good choices for the math center while appointment books might be best utilized in the dramatic play center. Beyond these center-specific items, all centers need to have three types of print—books and resources, environmental print, and purposeful print.

Reading and writing development are fostered as children interact naturally with the first type of print, books and other reading materials. Everything children learn about print through reading benefits them as writers, and different types of text offer unique learning potential. Therefore, a plentiful supply of books from all genres of literature should be present. These books, both commercial and child-written, reflect a wide range of ages, interests, cultures, reading levels, and developmental abilities. Classic as well as contemporary fiction and nonfiction books should be selected to cover an array of topics in science, art, social studies, math, and music while exposing children to the vast alternatives for illustrating literature. In addition to trade books, classrooms should contain magazines, plays, poetry, newspapers, reference books, conceptual books, wordless picture books, predictable books, environmental print books, and picture dictionaries. Through interactions with many types of printed materials, children will expand their language and thinking skills by learning to use written language in different forms that meet different needs.

While the library/listening center is the most obvious place to store books and other reading materials, it is recommended that at least four books per child be distributed in different areas throughout the remainder of the classroom (Morrow 1990). Nature and science books are perfect for the discovery center while books depicting construction and building can inspire imaginative construction in the block center. The biography of a famous artist with accompanying examples of his work makes an appealing and informative display for the art center.

Attention should be drawn to print that occurs naturally within the environment. Signs on restrooms and exits are examples of typical classroom environmental print as well as brand names and models on items such as the computer. Product names, logos or emblems, and sayings displayed on children's shoes and clothing are other types of environmental print found in classrooms.

Children learn a lot through reading environmental print (McGee, Lomax, and Head 1988; Neuman and Roskos 1993). Key objects in classrooms, such as door, window, and desk can be identified with a prominently displayed printed name, and preschool children in these classrooms will frequently use the labels and signs as a reference for writing during play (Neuman and Roskos 1990). It has also been found that children incorporate literacy into their play to enhance their pretend situations when the environment is rich with print (Morrow 1990; Neuman and Roskos 1997; Vukelich 1994).

Purposeful print, the third type of print, provides information directly pertaining to the context in which it is found. Examples of purposeful print include posted information related to the current day, special events, or classroom functioning as well as signs and directions. Posting purposeful print such as calendars, menus, notices, announcements, and daily schedules displays pertinent information while allowing children to value writing and its many functions.

Christopher uses magnetic letters to spell the names of classmates.

Written instructions for classroom procedures, from hand washing to operating a tape recorder or logging onto a computer, provide helpful reminders, authentic reasons for reading, and easily accessible models for writing (Routman 1991; Schuele, Roberts, Fitzgerald, and Moore 1993; Taylor, Blum, and Logsdon 1986).

In addition to providing a print-rich environment, supplies and equipment for recording language must also be present. Pencils, pens, paper, journals, observation logs, message boards, chalkboards, blank books, tape recorders, video cameras, computers, and other materials for recording oral and written language should be available throughout the classroom for children's use. These supplies and equipment promote communication within the classroom, increase fluency in writing, and enhance children's self-esteem (Routman 1991). A message center or class mailbox system encourages and organizes written communication between teachers and children or between children themselves (Routman 1991; Taylor, Blum, and Logsdon 1986) while a daily report or weekly newsletter written or dictated by children facilitates communication between school and home.

Developing Fine Motor Skills

During the preschool years, young children develop the ability to use their fingers to manipulate objects. These fine motor skills become more precise when children are given the opportunity to manipulate objects in meaningful ways. Manipulating objects includes practice in grasping, releasing, inserting, assembling, or disassembling and increases tactile awareness. Traditional preschool activities such as putting pegs in pegboards, stringing beads, and working puzzles are as important as ever for improving children's fine motor skills. As children paint with large paintbrushes, color on blank paper, and use scissors, muscles in the fingers are strengthened and developed. Dressing themselves also involves the use of fine motor skills as children button large buttons, use snaps and zippers, and pull on socks and tie shoes. These self-help skills can be fostered in the classroom by providing costumes, dressing frames, or dolls. Teachers provide encouragement and, when needed, assistance as children master these and other new skills using developing muscles in the fingers and hands. Figure 3–1 offers specific suggestions for assisting children in mastering fine motor skills.

Since fine motor skills are still developing in prekindergarten, children's handwriting is much different from that of school-age children. Young children initially handle writing instruments using a fist grip in which their palm is wrapped around the pencil. Their hand and arm do not rest on the writing surface, and the muscles in the upper arm, rather than in the fingers, are used to

Figure 3–1 *Supporting children's fine motor development*

Developmental Area	Activity(ies)
shoulder and wrist muscles	write on vertical surface, such as a chalkboard or easel
finger manipulation and dexterity	squirt a spray bottle, lift small items with tweezers, and use manipulatives, such as buttons, beads, and Unifix® cubes
pincer grip	pop plastic "bubbles" on packing sheets, open and close sealable plastic bags, snap snaps, wind up toys that have a knob, use an eye dropper or tweezers, spin tops, use large plastic needles to sew yarn into pieces of burlap, tear paper, and use scissors
finger strength and control	use a hole-punch, push golf tees into clay, cut cardboard, and lift small objects with tweezers
fine motor control	use games that involve spatial construction, such as Legos®, Tinkertoys®, Lincoln Logs™, and other blocks
tactile/kinesthetic awareness	draw large letters in the air, write with finger in shaving cream or finger paint

move the pencil. This results in large markings made randomly on the paper. With greater development of fine motor skills, children rest their wrist on the table and learn to rotate it while maintaining the fist grip on the pencil. This results in smaller marks on the paper. Gradually, children hold the pencil in their fingers, rest the side of their hand on the surface, and use their fingers to control the movement. This produces finer marks and smaller print placed strategically on the paper.

Because of the gradual development of children's handwriting skills, it is recommended that the formation of letters and emphasis on handwriting be delayed until at least first grade. Forcing children to repeat a skill they are not physically ready to do can have a damaging effect. Requiring four year olds, for example, to write on lined paper will discourage them from wanting to write at all. As an alternative, teachers of young children can capitalize on children's interest in drawing and experimenting with writing instruments by providing children with a variety of marking materials and a supply of large sheets of blank paper. Working on a vertical surface, such as a chalkboard or easel, helps develop strength in the shoulder and wrist muscles, which are needed for writing.

When children do begin using fine motor skills to make letters, it is recommended that they be allowed to experiment with how letters are formed as

Using salt as a writing medium allows messages to be erased quickly and easily.

they gain confidence in using writing to express meaning (Tompkins 2004). A teacher can step in and demonstrate a simpler way to form a specific letter if the child is experiencing difficulty writing it in his own way. Formal instruction, such as handwriting practice worksheets, should not be introduced. Instead, young children (in prekindergarten) should practice handwriting within the context of real writing experiences.

Playing with sand, water, flour, rice, corn meal, gravel, or other sensory materials allows children to refine their coordination and develop new approaches for using the marking instruments. Consider using sand or flour on the tabletop, in a cookie sheet, or on a colored tray as an alternative writing medium (Wellhousen and Crowther 2004). Children can make letters and words using fingers, craft sticks, or brushes. Written messages are erased quickly and easily, allowing for multiple attempts and quick revisions. Writing in finger paint, pudding, or shav-

Scooping and pouring rice offers fine motor and cognitive benefits.

ing cream provides other enjoyable options and—when sealed inside large, clear bags—limited mess.

In addition to the fine motor benefits, children's understanding of physical properties, mathematical concepts, and scientific principles improves when allowed to scoop, shovel, stir, sift, pour, and measure freely. This increased understanding is often the momentum for publishing, and the publishing opportunities provide the venue for exploring process-related vocabulary in print (that is, sieve, filter, funnel, mold, and flow).

■ Making It Public

Displaying children's pictures, dictated stories, or attempts at writing affirms children's status as users and creators of print by making them published authors (Schuele, Roberts, Fitzgerald, and Moore 1993). Children's projects with accompanying written explanations are exhibited prominently to reflect the amount of time and effort expended to build a skyscraper using blocks or paint a family portrait. Posting student-made signs, directions, and labels presents a practical publishing opportunity. Some signs will become permanent classroom fixtures, such as a reminder to turn off the lights when leaving the classroom. Others, such as an upcoming field trip announcement, will fill a temporary need and remain only a short time.

Teachers with limited wall space can string a clothesline for displaying children's work. They can also suspend clothespins from the ceiling using clear fishing line to create hanging displays or use them for attaching papers to window blinds. Bulletin board borders can be used to outline space on cabinet doors, restroom walls, or along the hallway to make mini bulletin boards or to transform the side of a filing cabinet into a magnetic display space. The tops of bookcases and windowsills make excellent show places for three-dimensional projects.

Self-selected work from all children can be displayed, and displays can be kept current by rotating work on exhibit every two weeks. When children are given the opportunity to choose and display their own work, it will be exhibited at the child's own eye level and produce a child-centered atmosphere that commercial decorations are unable to duplicate. Giving children ownership of display space also increases their pride in and responsibility for the room's appearance while freeing adults from what can become a cumbersome task. As with the work itself, perfection in the display is not expected. The displays that children create confirm that teachers value children's best possible efforts.

Displaying children's writing is only one of many options available for publishing their stories. Allowing children to make their writing available for others to read and enjoy serves as strong motivation not only to write more but to also improve their writing. Each learning center needs to provide a way for children to share with adults and peers through writing what they know or have learned. Whether it's evaluating a website in the computer center directory, noting observations of pet activity in the discovery center, recording a block structure using a pocket chart with cards, or depicting number sets in a math center counting book, publishing is essential for supporting and sustaining emerging writers. Repeated and varied publishing experiences encourage and enable these budding writers by creating a perception of themselves as authors while providing immediate recognition and affirmation of their effort.

Dictating Oral Anecdotes

Publishing Children's First Stories

4

If a story is in you, it has to come out.
　　　　　—William Faulkner

When my son Jackson was seven years old, he had a serious bicycle accident that required a trip to the emergency room and ten stitches in his right knee. This ordeal had a strong emotional impact on him (and his parents), and he chose to write a book about the experience as a way to tell his classmates exactly what happened when he was well enough to return to school. Jackson knew *how* to write, but his previous writing experiences had been limited to one-page stories accompanied by a single illustration. The prospect of writing a whole book with all the details he wanted to include was overwhelming. So, I offered to serve as a scribe, carefully taking down each word until he would point and say, "Stop here, so I can draw the picture later." The result was a published piece written beyond what Jackson would have attempted on his own. His view of himself as a writer was elevated when he saw his words published in a whole book and read it aloud to his classmates.

We have defined publishing as making available what you know to others through writing. Publishing gives writers, regardless of their age or ability, a purpose for writing. When stories are published and shared with others, they become something special and give the author a sense of pride and accomplishment. This is why Lucy Calkins (1994) says publication is "the *beginning*, not the *culmination of* the writing process." Through publishing, children are inducted into being an author and experience the sense of accomplishment associated with this achievement. As a result, they are motivated to publish regularly and gradually become more independent in their ability to write.

Dictated anecdotes is a strategy used to introduce children to the concept that writing is a useful way to record what they have to say. As we take dictation for children telling stories, they observe that text is simply speech written down. Over time, they begin to understand that when their stories are written down, they can be enjoyed again and again. Making the connection between speech and text is crucial to reading and writing development.

Recording children's anecdotes in written form is a developmentally appropriate way to introduce children to writing because they are natural storytellers. Typically, their stories take the form of anecdotes as they give an oral account of an event they have experienced, witnessed, or even imagined. Often, a story is told about a drawing or painting in which they have attempted to represent an object or event of interest. The primary concern of young children is to get their story out in order to share their thoughts. Initially, young children are not concerned with recording their stories. In fact, they are unaware that written records help people remember and share past experiences (Schickedanz and Casbergue 2004). Their objective is to simply share their thoughts in the immediate moment. This narrow cognitive perspective is consistent with Piaget's (1975) description of the preoperational thinker. Children at this level of cognitive development are egocentric in their thinking and are interested first and foremost in getting their own needs met. In this case, the need is to communicate.

The teacher plays an important role in the dictated anecdotes strategy. Specifically, the teacher helps children understand that their oral anecdotes have value. Because young children's concepts of time and history are limited, they don't realize the value of recording stories is they can be enjoyed again later or with others who were not present for the original telling. Children do not naturally comprehend the benefits of written language, so they need multiple experiences in order to understand its purposes. When teachers make a written record of anecdotes and read them aloud so children can hear their own words, they are introducing the concept and purpose of writing and increasing the children's awareness of the value of writing. As teachers establish venues for sharing recorded stories with others, children witness an audience's reaction to their writing and, as a result, are motivated to have more anecdotes recorded.

When we observe a group of young children and listen to their conversation, it quickly becomes apparent that they have plenty to say and are rarely shy about saying it! Their conversations are often surprising and humorous because young children are uninhibited enough to share whatever is on their minds at

Ms. Liz takes dictation as Jay tells a story about his drawing.

the moment. It is their enthusiasm for talking and sharing stories that makes dictated anecdotes a useful strategy for introducing writing to young children.

■ Characteristics of Learners

Children who, for a variety of reasons, are not yet able to communicate independently in writing benefit from the dictated anecdotes strategy. More proficient writers, such as teachers and parents, serve as scribes who write down what children say as they say it. Children who benefit from this strategy include emergent and beginning writers, children with special needs, and English language learners (ELLs).

Emergent and Beginning Writers

Young children with very limited understanding of print are considered emergent writers. They experiment with writing by making random marks on paper (Clay 1991; Schickedanz 1990; Sulzby 1992). Because they do not use sound-symbol relationships in their writing, it is unreadable to others. Teachers of emergent writers use dictated anecdotes to provide children with a model of how writing works. As the child tells her oral anecdote, she watches the teacher write it on paper. Then the story is read back to the child, so she understands that her exact words are being recorded in a written form.

Beginning writers are children with a basic knowledge of sound-symbol relationships whose writing is often decipherable. While their spelling is far from conventional, they use letters to represent sounds efficiently enough that their writing can be read by others. Because these children communicate through writing, they benefit from the dictated anecdotes strategy when they want to attempt a writing project that is beyond their independent ability. This situation occurs when their fine motor skills, attention span, or understanding of print are not developed enough to write the story they want to convey and they need someone to serve as a scribe. This was the situation in the opening vignette about Jackson and his bicycle accident.

Children with Special Needs

Children with special needs, such as visual impairment, hearing loss, learning disabilities, speech and language disorders, impaired motor skills, and mild cognitive delays, benefit from having their oral stories recorded as well. Like all children, those with special needs have stories and experiences to share. By dictating ideas to another, their thoughts are efficiently recorded to be enjoyed again later or shared with an audience. For these children, recording stories serves as a confidence builder and an encouraging reminder of what they *can* do.

English Language Learners

Some children may have difficulty writing their own stories due to language barriers. English language learners (ELLs) account for more than three million students in the United States (NCELA/National Clearinghouse for English Language Acquisition & Language Instruction Educational Programs 2003). Children who are learning to speak English as their second language face many obstacles in communicating, both orally and in writing. Putting ideas on paper offers a special challenge because they must first determine how to translate their ideas into English and then know the symbols that represent the sounds in the words. In addition, ELLs are learning punctuation and other conventions of print. The support of a scribe makes it possible for ELLs to have their ideas recorded as they learn these skills. Language development is further facilitated as the scribe reads back the story that has been written in English.

▮ Taking Dictation

Dictation can be taken in different ways depending on the purpose and the context for writing. Typically, the child's word choice and grammar are preserved even if it is in nonstandard English. Teachers sometimes use quotation marks to denote that children's speech is recorded verbatim. This convention creates an important distinction when a child's anecdote is told with grammatical errors or surprising facts. It is important to record children's exact language to ensure that the child can read what is written and to create a record of the child's oral language ability. It is also necessary for the teacher to identify errors being made as those of the child. Quotation marks serve this function.

Taking dictation accomplishes three distinct functions. First, it introduces children to the speech-to-text connection. Second, it enables children to accomplish more as writers than would be possible when writing independently. Third, it serves as a model for the conventions of print.

Introduce the Speech-to-Text Connection

With repeated experiences of dictated anecdotes, children begin to make mental connections between oral and written language and gradually begin to realize that print is written speech. This realization is a significant moment in the lives of young writers. It serves as a great motivator for developing the skills needed to write independently. Understanding that print is speech written down is considered social arbitrary knowledge (Piaget 1975), meaning children cannot construct this concept on their own. They must be shown the concept and have repeated experiences in an authentic setting to understand it.

Provide Support

Emerging writers, ambitious beginning writers, children with special needs, and ELLs need adults to record their oral anecdotes. This serves as a "scaffold" (Bruner 1992) so they can achieve a goal at a level beyond what they could accomplish independently. Lev Vygotsky (1962/1986) refers to the zone of proximal development, or ZPD, the range of abilities between what the child can do independently and what he can achieve with the help of a more proficient individual. Each group of children identified is moved beyond their current knowledge and ability level with the support of a scribe who records their oral anecdotes. Scaffolding children so they can achieve goals beyond what they accomplish independently is considered a powerful method for working with emergent writers (Tompkins 2005), children with special needs (Klein, Cook, and Richardson-Gibbs 2001), and ELLs (Sutterby 2005).

Model Conventions of Print

When children see their own words in written form, they are introduced to conventions of writing in a meaningful way. Marie Clay (1975) identified a set of principles young children notice about writing and eventually incorporate into their own early attempts to write. These include:

- Recurring principle. The same shapes are used over and over in writing.

- Sign concept. Print is different from pictures in that letters do not look like the object represented by the word created with them.

- Flexibility principle. Letters may be written differently but the direction the letter faces remains the same.

- Page-arrangement principle. Writing is made up of lines of print written from left to right and top to bottom.

Taking dictation helps children develop these principles as well as word awareness, spelling, and the conventions of written language (Bissex 1980; Clay 1979).

■ Publishing Dictated Anecdotes from Morning Share Time

Traditionally, early childhood teachers begin the school day with a whole-group meeting time in which the children gather on a rug or carpet squares to discuss the calendar, weather, and attendance. During this routine, children also participate in morning share time in which they orally tell about personal experiences. Rather than just listening to children, the teacher records each child's comments on a chart pad resting on an easel or chalkboard tray. Observing the teacher write their exact message as spoken helps children understand the connection between written and oral language.

During morning share time, the teacher asks the class, "Who has something interesting to share?" and calls on five to eight children each day, depending on the attention span of the group and length of time spent sharing. The morning share time chart serves as a record for who has shared throughout the week. The teacher can use previous charts to determine who shares most often and to ensure that each child has an opportunity to contribute an oral anecdote. Or, the teacher may designate ahead of time which children will share each day to ensure that every child has an opportunity to provide an oral anecdote throughout the week.

When selected, the child shares a brief anecdote with the class orally. If the child has a longer anecdote to share, after allowing him to finish, the teacher asks, "What is the most important part of what you just told us?" The teacher then records what the child has said verbatim in large letters on a chart pad. She may do this by writing the child's name followed by a colon and then the anecdote written verbatim, or by writing the child's name and the anecdote in quotes.

The teacher continues this procedure until the time allotted for morning share time is over or a predetermined number of anecdotes has been recorded. Then the teacher reads aloud each contributor's name and their sentence, while running her hand under the words to draw children's attention to the text and show left-to-right progression. The chart is dated and the intact chart pad is placed in the writing center or some other prominent area where children can review it during the day. In addition to serving as a source for readable text and a model for writing, the morning share time chart is used to recall topics children have shared in the past. A morning share time chart might read something like this:

Brianna: My mom throwed up this morning. The baby in her tummy makes her feel sick.

Max: Me and my dad watched baseball on T.V.

Ryan: I had to eat lasagna for dinner, and it was yucky.

Or the teacher may use quotes to delineate the child's exact speech:

Brittany said, "My grandma called and said she is coming to visit next week."

Chase said, "My next-door neighbor fell off his trampoline and broked his arm!"

Will said, "We was late to school because my dog got out the fence."

Notice that each child contributed a rich, unique anecdote that expressed an event that was on his or her mind at the moment. Morning share time is different from other forms of morning message routines because each child is encouraged to contribute his own original thought. Other formats of morning message give children a specific topic to talk about or a question to answer, such as "Name something that smells good" or "What did you eat for breakfast?" It

William uses a pointer as the class reads the chart written in morning share time.

is important that children share their own personal anecdotes rather than respond to a predetermined question or topic. If children are to become competent writers, they must learn that what they have to share is valuable.

■ Publishing Dictated Anecdotes from Stories Children Tell

There are many ways to publish children's oral anecdotes when you keep in mind our broad definition of publishing. A dictated story accompanied by a related drawing made by the child makes it more personally meaningful. A child's explanation of an encounter with an armadillo in her backyard is considered published when the teacher takes dictation at the computer and prints the page for the child to illustrate and place in the library center. A self-portrait accompanied by a dictated paragraph titled "All About Heather" is considered published when it is laminated and taped to the back of the author's desk for Open House. Children are publishing when their verbal descriptions of a favorite food are written down and posted on the bulletin board in the cafeteria. Children's stories are also published when they sit in the author's chair and share a drawing and dictated anecdote about their birthday party. Opportunities for publishing children's oral anecdotes are limited only by the imaginations of the authors and teachers. Additional ideas for publishing children's anecdotes include:

- Read dictated anecdotes to older "buddy readers" from upper-grade classrooms.

- Celebrate the writing accomplishments of one child by posting dictated anecdotes with an accompanying photo on a bulletin board designated for this purpose.

- Record children's dictated anecdotes on cassette tape to be placed in the listening center.

- Send home children's dictated anecdotes in a folder designated for this purpose with a page attached requesting "reviews" from the child's family.

- Place children's dictated anecdotes in page protectors and organize in a three-ring binder.

Children's anecdotes can be published regardless of whether they are dictated during whole-group or small-group settings, or on an individual basis. We have provided specific suggestions for recording children's oral anecdotes during whole-group meetings typically scheduled at the start of each school day. We have labeled this routine "morning share time." Ideas for recording children's oral anecdotes as they work in centers, either in small groups or alone, are also presented.

◼ Publishing Dictated Anecdotes in Learning Centers

Learning center time provides a good opportunity to record children's oral anecdotes, either in small groups or individually, while they are engaged in a variety of activities. In centers, children are involved in activities that are of interest to them. While engaged in these activities, children take on dramatic play roles, use their imaginations, participate in negotiations, learn to share, and engage in decision making. Their choices range from making a collage to solving a puzzle or pretending to be a storybook character, all in the span of a single morning. These varied experiences give children much to think, talk, and tell about, which makes centers an ideal time for recording oral anecdotes.

Dramatic play offers numerous publishing opportunities.

Children are encouraged to write their own messages in centers where paper, pencils, and print are available (see Chapter 3). Studies consistently show the benefits of making drawing and writing materials accessible so young children can experiment with print as they play (Neuman and Roskos 1990; Vukelich 1990). Teachers heighten children's attention to these materials when they demonstrate how they can be used by recording the speech children use while at play. In the block center, the teacher records children's accounts of a building they constructed in a block center journal. The teacher takes dictation for a child who wants to give an oral "book report" after listening to an audiotape of *My Lucky Day* (Kasza 2003) in the library center. Another child tells his own version of this story as the teacher takes dictation in a blank book, leaving space for the child to illustrate. After watching a puppet show, the teacher records some of the lines used by the children in speech bubbles of various sizes and shapes that are printed on a page (Solley 2005). In the discovery center, a child describes a fossil examined with a magnifying glass while the teacher takes dictation using an observation form attached to a clipboard. After observing the teacher use writing materials for different purposes, children will begin to emulate the teacher's writing behavior as they experiment with writing in centers.

Julia describes her castle for the block journal.

Teachers who value children's oral language plan for opportunities to record dictated anecdotes throughout the day, such as during morning share time or at centers. They also stay alert for impromptu opportunities to jot down on paper children's interesting, creative, and humorous perceptions of the world around them. Publishing these fleeting moments that would have otherwise been lost introduces children to the meaning and value of writing.

5 | Translating Kid Writing

Publishing Children's First Written Stories

I admire anyone who has the guts to write anything at all.

—E. B. White

Jackson joined a neighborhood swim team for the first time at the age of nine. A few other children were new to the team, but most had swum competitively, some since the age of four. It was interesting to see the range of abilities exhibited by the children during those first weeks of swim practice. But what intrigued me more were the intuitive teaching abilities of the young swim coaches, Susanna and Rachel, both college students with competitive swimming experience. They related to the children in a supportive and respectful manner, and their approach built naturally on the children's interests and individual strengths as swimmers.

First, the children never had to sit on the sides listening to instruction or watching someone else swim. They began practice by letting each child jump off the swim block into the pool to swim laps, accommodating the children's natural desire to be in the water. Second, rather than focusing on only one stroke or kick until it was perfected, the children practiced the whole range of swim strokes they would eventually be using in competition. For the beginners, this meant exposure to six or more new strokes and kicks at once, and all were practiced every day. Third, the coaches carefully watched each child swim and gave specific and immediate feedback as needed. They continued to observe the swimmer to ensure that the correction was made. Within a few short weeks, every swim team member, regardless of experience, demonstrated great progress and exhibited a love for the sport.

If teachers were to follow the lead of these young swim coaches, we could provide this same successful experience for young writers. We must respect and build on what they already know about communicating through print. Children should be allowed to jump into writing rather than being required to sit and listen to instruction that is unrelated to what they are trying to accomplish. Children will be encouraged to "splash around" with whatever skills they may possess as writers, whether it is just scribbling in a line or copying words from a sign. Finally, we must provide feedback and correction that is relevant to what they are writing at the moment.

▪ Spontaneous Forms of Writing

Spontaneous forms of writing appear when children make their first attempts to communicate through writing. These writing forms are commonly referred to as "kid writing," to help children understand that their writing is allowed to look different from adults' writing (Tompkins 2005). As a result of observing the functions and forms of writing used by adults, children develop an awareness of the purpose of writing, evidenced by the onset of early writing, their kid writing. Even though a clear message is not always evident from early attempts at writing, the effort should be recognized. Much like the child who attempts actual speech by reaching for his father and saying "da-da," early attempts and approximations of writing are also cause for celebration.

Young children have been found to use different forms of spontaneous kid writing, including drawing, scribbles, letterlike forms, letter strings, conventional spelling, and invented spelling (Sulzby 1985; Sulzby 1992; Sulzby, Barnhart, and Heishima 1989). In addition, we have added a seventh form, "environmental printing," which includes conventional forms of print copied from the environment, such as a classroom display or the cover of a book.

The spontaneous forms of writing used by emerging writers are not stages and do not occur in a sequence. Children use different forms under varying circumstances and may combine forms by incorporating conventionally spelled words among invented spellings (Morrow 1996; Sulzby 1986). Their choice of writing may be based on the message to be conveyed, knowledge of letter sounds, ability to form specific letters, knowledge of memorized standard spellings, and availability of print in the environment. The result is writing that is personally meaningful and can be read by the child but may be unreadable to others.

Drawing

Often, young children do not differentiate between drawing and writing and see the two behaviors as synonymous. When children use drawing, also called "picture writing," as a means of telling a story, they are working out the similarities and differences between the two methods of communicating (Morrow 2005b). Both involve using paper and a marking instrument, such as a crayon or pencil, to produce a symbol for an object or idea. However, pictures are a realistic symbol while writing uses abstract symbols. Children who use drawings as a way to write often "read" their pictures with the tone and intonation used when reading a story aloud. An example of using drawing as a way to communicate through writing can be found in Figure 5–1.

Figure 5–1 *Example of using* drawing *as a way to write.*

Scribble-writing

While scribble-writing may look like manuscript, it usually resembles adult cursive writing (Schickedanz 1986), and we distinguish it from the scribbles made in early drawings because, instead of circular or aimless marks, scribble-writing creates horizontal lines, indicating the child's understanding that writing is different from drawing (Beatty 2006). Giving this form of writing an alternate name when introducing it to children, such as loop-de-loop, helps create a distinction between scribble-writing and the negatively perceived scribbles produced by very young children (Wood 1999).

Children using scribble-writing are convinced that they are writing like adults and, therefore, believe that their scribbles can be read. It is common for a child to ask an adult to read their scribble-writing aloud to them, so they will know what they have written (see Figure 5–2).

Figure 5–2 *Examples of using* scribble-writing *as a way to write.*

Figure 5–3 *Example of using* letterlike forms *as a way to write.*

Letterlike Forms

The marks used for scribble-writing gradually become more defined and begin taking on the appearance of manuscript letters with straight, curved, and intersecting lines (Schickedanz 1982). Horizontal lines of letterlike forms have also been labeled "mock writing" (Temple, Nathan, Temple, and Burris 1993). These original forms that resemble actual letters are intentional, not just letters that have been formed incorrectly (see Figure 5–3). Letterlike forms are evidence of progress in the child's writing development (Clay 1975). Analysis of children's mock letter writing reveals they are learning the following concepts consistent with the formation of real letters: symmetry, uniformity of size and shape, inner complexity, left-to-right directionality, linearity, and appropriate placement (Hayes 1990).

Letter Strings

Another form of spontaneous writing consists of strings of letters and numbers, which may contain errors in orientation (facing the wrong direction) and in form (formed using the wrong number of lines). Reversing the direction of letters is typical when children begin to write since the direction an object faces often makes no difference in identifying the object (Beatty 2006). A coffee mug

The rain makes the flower grow.

Figure 5–4 *Example of using* letter strings *as a way to write.*

remains the same object regardless of which direction the handle faces or if it is upside down. With experience, children learn that this generality does not apply to letters. In the meantime, correctly identifying and producing the letters *d*, *b*, *p*, and *q* remains a challenge but not a cause of concern.

When writing letter strings, children demonstrate accuracy in spacing by forming letters without them touching one another (Schickedanz 1986). They may show a preference for letters they know well, such as the ones in their name, and repeat them in a random order. This form of writing shows children's emerging awareness of letter forms and how they are used in writing (see Figure 5–4 for an example of using letter strings as a way to communicate through writing).

Figure 5–5 *Examples of using* conventional spelling *as a way to write.*

Conventional Spelling

Young children memorize the spelling of words that hold special meaning for them, such as their own name. In addition to their own name, they may know how to spell the names of classmates, their names for parents ("Mom"), and words such as "love," "dog," and "cat." They may also use often-seen high frequency words, such as "my," "I," "am," and "is." Young children will typically write words that they have memorized in a line without leaving spaces between the words. When encouraged to leave spaces between words, they will often fill the blanks with a symbol such as a heart or star. As they learn more about conventions of writing, they begin to leave spaces between conventionally spelled words. Words that are memorized, and therefore spelled conventionally, will emerge among words written in other forms, such as invented spellings (see Figure 5–5).

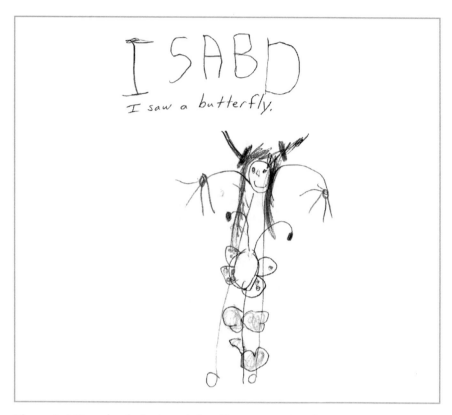

I saw a butterfly.

Figure 5–6 *Examples of using* invented spelling *as a way to write.*

Invented Spelling

Learning to spell is like learning other new tasks. It is developmental and occurs in stages. In the earliest stages, children are dependent on the sounds they hear in a word. When children make the important connection between the sounds they hear in a word and the letters that represent them, they make their first attempts to spell. This approximation at spelling is called invented spelling because children are devising their own unique way of spelling based on the sounds they hear and recognize in words (see Figure 5–6). At first, children represent a whole word or syllable with just one letter, usually the letter that represents the first sound they hear in the word. As children recognize more sounds in the word, these are also represented. Typically, first and final consonant sounds are represented followed by the addition of long vowels. Consonants that represent more than one sound

I
WL
Hav
tre
For
\X
9vn
ME MFv
HALS

"I will have turkey
for Thanksgiving at
Mimi's house."

(Figure 5–6) *continued*

and short vowel sounds appear later. Teachers can suggest children "stretch" the words as they say them (pronounce the word slowly), to help them identify more sounds in the words they want to spell.

Children use creative substitutions for sounds that are less recognizable. The word "the" is a challenge and often spelled as "v" or "de". Substituting "ch" for "tr" is also common for inventive spellers ("truck" is spelled "c-h-r-u-k). Teachers can bring children's attention to standard spelling used in the environment or in books to help them learn how to spell these non-phonetic words.

As children have more and more opportunities to write using invented spelling, they begin representing enough sounds that their writing can be read even though it is not spelled conventionally. For example, a child attempting to write "I prayed for all the soldiers" may inventively spell the sentence in this way, "I prad for ol v sogers." The initial use of invented spellings is a pivotal period in the development of a young writer and is an important step toward

I'm da tebol and ron and
ron and ron I hit the
Bol and ron to the Besis
Pabb hlp my teBol to not
lus and help Me Brg
Betr at My teBol

(Figure 5–6) *continued*

standard spelling. Feeling capable and confident is necessary for young children to continue taking risks with their invented spelling.

Environmental Printing

Young children's initial reading experiences often begin with a multitude of models of environmental print provided by the classroom, home, and community environments (Harste, Woodward, and Burke 1984). The positive response they receive for this accomplishment reinforces future attempts at reading print from the environment. As a result, children become very aware of the print around them and begin incorporating print from the environment into their own writing. Teachers can support children's experimentation with environmental print by providing models for them to use. Labeling objects around the room, creating a bulletin board display of pictures with word labels, and word walls (lists of words written in alphabetized sections) are ideal for providing useful models of environmental printing.

Children use environmental printing to write in three very different ways. First, they may simply copy print from their immediate environment with no regard for word selection or meaning. For example, Brooke, a kindergartener, wants to write a note to her older sister in second grade. She knows from previous attempts that her scribbles and letter strings do not convey a message that her sister can read, a limitation her sister is only too glad to point out. So, Brooke uses actual words from around the classroom. Carefully, she copies each word as it is written, resulting in a message like, "Monday Tuesday November word wall days of school helper of the week."

Another way emergent writers use environmental printing is as an inspiration for new topics. One day, while searching for a new topic, Alexandria looked around the classroom and spotted her lunchbox on the shelf. After making several trips from her seat to the shelf, Alexandria successfully copied the word *Barbie* into her journal. Barbie remained the focus of her journal entries over the next few days as she continued to expand on this topic.

A third, more sophisticated way emergent writers use environmental printing is to help them spell correctly an actual word they want to use in their message. For example, six-year-old Michael was making a list of pet supplies he needed for his new hamster. Using the food container of the class pet as a model, he copied the text, "Gerbil Food Pellets." Christopher used environmental printing in this way as he incorporated the title from a book he had read into a journal entry where other forms of kid writing were used. He wrote, "I red if you give a mouse a cookie ol bi misef" [I read If You Give a Mouse a Cookie all by myself]. Figure 5–7 includes examples of using environmental printing as a way to communicate through writing.

■ Introducing Kid Writing

Teachers support children's writing by providing examples of the different forms of kid writing and introducing them at a pace based on children's attention span and interest in learning ways to write. They may present them all at once or demonstrate them gradually (Wood 1999).

Rosa, a prekindergarten teacher, introduced her children to different forms of kid writing by conducting brief minilessons during their morning circle time. Once a week, over several weeks, she demonstrated the forms of writing typi-

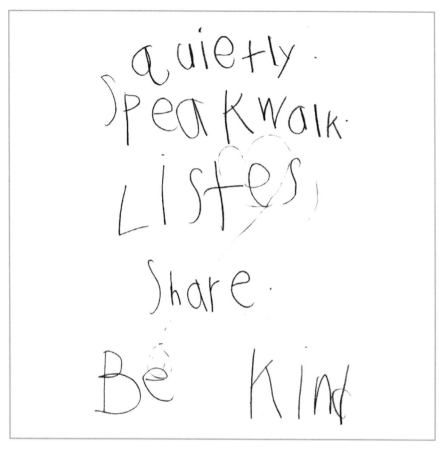

Figure 5–7 *Examples of using environmental print as a way to write. The list of class rules is copied from the board.*

cally used by emergent writers, beginning with "drawing." On a large poster board she printed the word *drawing* on the left side and then demonstrated how she would make a message to represent the sentence, "I brought my lunch to school" by drawing a picture of herself carrying a lunchbox. She explained to the children, this is one way to write a message. The next week, Rosa introduced "scribble-writing" by labeling the example with the printed word, *scribble* and then making a series of loops as she said the words, "I brought my lunch to school," adding the example to the poster board. The following week, the letter string form of writing was introduced in which Rosa wrote random letters on the chart while stating the sentence aloud.

The process of introducing the remaining writing forms to children with examples continued over several weeks. When the invented spelling form was taught to her children, Rosa placed emphasis on the first (and sometimes the

Dis BiBIe With atoo

"This is Barbie with a tatoo."

(**Figure 5–7** *continued*) *The word* Barbie *is copied from a lunchbox, and invented and conventional spellings are incorporated.*

final) letter sound in each word. She asked the children to help her think of the letter that represented the sound emphasized. As she wrote the conventional form of the sentence, Rosa explained to the children that she knew how these words were spelled because she has written them so many times before. She asked the children to name words that they already know how to spell to ensure they understand the concept as presented.

Finally, Rosa introduced copying words from the environment. The children looked around the classroom and found the words from print in their classroom environment, "my," "lunchbox," "to," and "school." The children told her to write the letter *I* for the first word. Rosa asked how she should fill in the word *brought*. The children suggested she use another form of writing such as loop-de-loop or invented spelling.

(**Figure 5–7** *continued*) *The title of a book is copied into the child's reading log.*

After the series of minilessons on forms of kid writing was complete, the poster board chart was hung in the classroom for children to use as a reference. When they showed interest in adding print to their drawings or writing a message, Rosa would refer to the poster to remind children of the different ways they can communicate on paper through writing.

■ Under Writing

Teachers encourage young writers by responding to kid writing with the understanding that it contains a meaningful message. When children first begin experimenting with writing as a way to record ideas, the teacher can respond by helping children tell or "read" what they have written. As the child reads her attempt at writing, the teacher serves as a scribe, just as earlier she took dictation for the stories children told. This is done through a technique known as "under writing" in which the teacher writes under (or above) the child's attempt at writing. By providing a verbatim record of the child's message, under writing serves as a translation of kid writing. It is important to write the story exactly as it is told in order for children to be able to reread their message. As their writing and the accompanying under writing are shared with others, children will realize they play a critical role in getting their own thoughts on paper. This is a necessary concept for future writing development. (Examples of under writing can be seen in Figures 5–1 through 5–6.)

While under writing, teachers may use a cloze method technique in which letters that are familiar to the child are omitted from a word and a line is drawn to form a blank for him to fill in (see Figure 5–8). The teacher then helps the child determine what letter should be filled in. For example, a child writes, "I GO 2 PAGN AR SKL," and orally reads the message as "I'm going to the playground after school." As the teacher under writes, she leaves spaces for some of the letters that have been omitted: "I'm going _ _ the playgroun_ after sch_ _ l. The child then rereads his message and fills in the missing letters.

Curious about the difference between his own writing and the teacher's, the child may ask why it is necessary for the teacher to write the message since it is already recorded. The teacher offers a considerate reminder that while kid writing is acceptable for his age, using adult writing helps when sharing his

Figure 5–8 *Example of using the cloze method of under writing. Lines were drawn to help the child learn to spell "going" and "tomorrow" conventionally.*

message with others. The teacher can explain that in time, with more experience in writing, the child's writing will resemble that of adults and under writing will no longer be necessary. With consistent, similar explanations, children will trust and accept that under writing is a necessary but temporary procedure.

■ Publishing Kid Writing in Journals

Journals are an ideal format for recording children's kid writing. When journals are shared with others, they are a published product. Because journals are typically made of pages bound together, they resemble a book, conveying the idea that journals contain published pieces. Journals also record chronological evidence of children's writing, providing an invaluable source of assessment data over time. When reviewing entries, teachers, parents, and children can see developmental progress as it unfolds. Journals provide a record of how early forms of kid writing are gradually replaced with more sophisticated forms, such as invented and conventional spelling.

Various types of journals, including personal journals, dialogue journals, reading response journals, and learning logs, are appropriate for young children to use (Morrow 2005b). Because emerging writers are egocentric in nature, personal journals, resembling diaries in which children write about their daily lives and date the entries in chronological order, are a good first choice for young writers (Hannon 1999).

Journal formats differ as well. The teacher may staple a few pages inside construction-paper covers, place hole-punch paper inside a folder fastened with brads, or purchase spiral notebooks or other types of bound notebooks. Unlined paper is recommended for emerging writers because unlined paper encourages children to use the whole page to experiment with making marks, allowing them to progress from random scribbling to horizontal scribbling, an indication that they recognize the difference between drawing and writing. Lined paper may inhibit emerging writers' exploration of how writing works (Beatty 2006). Once children make the distinction between drawing and writing, the teacher can demonstrate how to draw a line across a page to divide it into two sections—one for drawing and one for writing. This is preferable to the lined paper used for handwriting practice.

Occasionally, young children's journal entries may become repetitive, drawing and telling about the same event over and over again. To the adult, the child may appear to be having difficulty thinking of new topics. However, this practice is similar to a child requesting that the same book be read repeatedly; when children hear repeat readings of a favorite book, they focus on different

Children write in their journals daily.

elements, learn new concepts each time it is read, and build confidence in themselves as readers (Holdaway 1979). When a child chooses the same journal topic repeatedly, the drawings and writings become more embellished. Also, repeated journal entries are typically the basis for children to go beyond drawing and write their first printed messages using a form of writing. Not only are repetitions normal, they serve a valuable purpose for the emergent writer (Hilliker 1988).

Journals are used to assess students' growth as writers. As teachers observe children incorporating a new form of writing, they can make a notation of this on the last page in the journal, labeled "Teacher Comments." Teachers can make similar notations when children begin using conventions of print, such as spacing and punctuation. The teacher comment page is also an excellent way to inform parents when children begin using sound-symbol correspondence as they attempt invented spellings. Teachers can note the actual date and words represented so parents can join in the celebration of this cognitive leap.

Megan uses a date stamp in her journal.

■ Recommendations for Daily Journal Writing

There are many variations of procedures for writing in journals, and teachers should make adjustments as needed to best meet the needs of their students. The following recommendations are based on research and the philosophy of writing presented throughout this text:

1. Schedule journal writing.

Time should be devoted to journal writing every day. When children write in journals daily over the span of a school year, journal entries become longer, with greater detail and fluency (Heller 1995). Journal writing should occur at a predictable time, such as the beginning of the school day.

2. Model journal writing.

Teachers should show students how to select topics and write in journals in front of the whole group. (This is especially important when journals are being introduced. When children become experienced at journal writing, daily modeling is not necessary.) The teacher can think aloud possible ideas such as,

"I could write about my cat and how she insists on sleeping on my pillow every night or about the school play that my son is in next week." After choosing a topic, she can draw a picture to correspond with it and then write on the topic using standard writing.

3. Encourage kid writing.

When children turn to the next blank page in their journal and begin to draw, they should be encouraged to use kid writing to tell about their picture. The teacher may refer to the chart depicting different forms of kid writing. Children can use a date stamp to record the date of the journal entry.

4. Take dictation and under write children's journal entries.

As children complete their journal entries, the teacher can take dictation for those drawing only a picture and under write for those using kid writing. If the child does not respond or seems unsure, the teacher can ask "What's happening here?" as she points to a portion of the picture.

After taking dictation, the teacher can read the story back to the child, pointing to each word as it is read and then invite the child to read the words aloud. The child's writing and adult writing should be compared to find similarities such as the same beginning letters, and the child should be praised for his attempts to write using pretend writing forms.

While waiting for the teacher to take dictation for others, children should be encouraged to look back through their journal at previous entries and try to read them. Other activities may be planned for students so they do not have to wait for the teacher. Students also may be given the option to put their journals in a basket marked "in progress" so they can go on to another activity. Throughout the day, the teacher can pull journals and take dictation until all are completed.

5. Provide time for sharing with peers.

Children need opportunities to share their journals with others. This may be done in a "pair share" activity in which two children take turns sharing with each other. Sharing may also be done in small groups with each child sitting at a table taking a turn reading her journal entry. Author's chairs can be used as a means for sharing journal entries. A specified number of children should share each day. This list may be prepared ahead of time so students will know when it is their day to share. In the author's chair, students should read their journal entry for the day and call on three students to ask follow-up questions or make positive comments about their work.

6. Share journals with families.

Periodically, journals can be sent home for families to read and return. It is helpful to include a note from the teacher explaining the purpose of the journal. An explanation of kid writing and examples of different forms should also be included. Family members may be invited to write positive comments on a response sheet attached for this purpose.

■ Encouraging Risk Taking in Reluctant Storytellers and Writers

Typically, children share their stories with others enthusiastically. However, children who are reluctant to do so need encouragement. Teachers must investigate the cause of any child's reluctance, which may range from shyness and feelings of inadequacy to a speech or hearing disability. With encouragement, appropriate methods for engaging children, and intervention (if necessary), the child should gradually begin to participate in oral storytelling and dictation activities.

Routine methods of talking with children about their finished products are often ineffective. If a teacher looks at a child's writing and asks, "What did you draw?" or "What did you write?" the child may be hurt when he thinks the content should be obvious. Or she may respond with only a two- or three-word phrase, like "That's my dog." Simply commenting on the product, such as "How nice" or "I like the colors you used," requires no response on the part of the child. Even the widely accepted approach of saying to the child, "Tell me about your picture," often results in static language—"It's the sun and clouds," rather than a story about what is happening in the drawing. Asking the appropriate questions is a crucial technique to helping children become comfortable sharing their stories.

Oken-Wright (1999) suggests that adults, when talking to children about their pictures, ask "What is happening here?" This question sets up an expectation that there is meaning behind the picture. The question can be asked several times in the single discussion of a drawing. As the child starts explaining what is happening in the picture, a story begins to emerge. For example:

Teacher: (Pointing to a gray animal) What's happening here?

Jackson: That's a rhino. He's playing basketball.

Teacher: (Pointing to a pink animal) What's happening here?

Jackson: That's a stinky pig. He plays for the other team.

Teacher: (Pointing to a ball hovering over a basket) What's happening here?

Jackson: Oh, the rhinos are playing against the stinky pigs. The rhinos just made a basket. And here is the scoreboard (pointing to another area on the page). The score is 21 to 0. The rhinos are the home team, and the stinky pigs are the visitor. They are going to lose. Rhinos rule!

This same technique can be used to encourage children to talk about their writing. As the teacher sits next to the child, points to the scribble-writing covering the top of the page, and asks, "What's happening here?" the child can share his intent. The response may be, "I was making smoke in the air," or he may reply, "That says, 'my dad got a new car.'" Asking the open-ended question, "What's happening here," does not insinuate that the teacher holds a particular expectation about the child's work. Instead, the question serves as a springboard to tell about her kid writing.

Some children wholeheartedly trust that kid writing is sufficient and without hesitation use spontaneous forms of writing with confidence. Others, however, may need more encouragement. The reasons for the difference between children vary. Children who have been encouraged to participate in authentic reading and writing experiences from a young age are enthusiastic about their personal abilities in regard to reading and writing. These children can be seen engaging in pretend reading with a familiar book and scribbling love notes to Mom and Dad with great confidence. Most likely, their close approximations to reading and writing behavior have always been recognized and reinforced.

The other extreme is the child who sits paralyzed at the teacher's suggestion that he write about a picture he has drawn. This child might have a highly developed awareness of right and wrong spellings and be reluctant to risk making a mistake. Children such as this become frustrated if adults refuse to provide conventional spellings for them and may refuse to participate in writing experiences. Graves (2003) labels children with this behavior and attitude as "perfectionists" who, with encouragement, will gradually attempt writing words they do not know how to spell.

Children may also exhibit reluctance to engage in writing experiences when they feel they are not as capable as peers. This may be the result of adults making inappropriate comparisons of children's written work or the misinterpretation of a teacher's comment toward another child's ability (Waring-Chaffee 1994). If they become uncomfortable or fearful that their attempts will be rejected, emergent writers will avoid activities that involve writing. Teachers can guard against this by remembering to avoid comparisons between children and their work and to use encouraging comments as a motivator.

The following guidelines summarize ways to enhance the literacy environment and encourage reluctant storytellers and writers (Waring-Chaffee 1994):

1. Create a classroom environment that provides opportunities for children to look and feel like writers.
2. Use literacy activities as a way to practice social experiences such as verbal and nonverbal exchanges.
3. Model writing and encourage children to participate without stipulating what their writing should look like.
4. Provide relevant literacy activities that maintain children's motivation and support their self-image as readers and writers.
5. Acknowledge children's approximations as they experiment with writing and use it in their play.

Observing children's spontaneous forms of writing is an interesting way to follow their development as writers. Translating kid writing into a conventional writing form preserves the integrity of their message while enabling others to read it. Daily journals provide a chronicle of what children learn and integrate into their writing over time.

6 Creating Cooperative Chronicles

Writing and Publishing with Peers

Writing is an exploration. You start from nothing and learn as you go.

—E. L. Doctorow

I n regard to my personal conception of how one person conveys information to another, I have all but replaced the term *teaching* with the word *scaffolding*. After many years observing and teaching children and adults, it has become apparent that learning occurs as a result of *interacting with* learners as opposed to dispensing information *to them* without their direct involvement. Take, for example, the task of teaching my teenage daughter to drive. Immediately after we got in the car and fastened our seatbelts, it was obvious that all the careful instructions I had given during breakfast that morning were totally useless. Once she was seated behind the wheel of the car, I realized by her glazed-over look that, although she had appeared to be listening by making eye contact and nodding at appropriate times while we were at the kitchen table, the information given had no real meaning. From the driver's seat, however, listening to my instruction was crucial to just backing down the driveway. With each driving session, I was able to give less instruction as she took on more responsibility for knowing how to drive. Finally, the day came when I stood nervously on the front porch watching her drive down the street on her own.

Teaching children to write requires the same process used to teach other tasks. We teach children by exposing them to the process of writing as well as its purpose—to publish and share their stories with others. Our goal is for them to be independent writers who understand both the necessity and the joy of writing. This is accomplished by providing support, or *scaffolding*, as needed and gradually letting go, allowing them to do more and more on their own.

■ Scaffolding Children's Writing

Revising is one of the most demanding aspects of writing, and it is important to introduce it in a way that makes sense to young writers. The teacher, instead of telling children what to do, should provide a scaffold by posing questions, asking for clarification, and making suggestions. The teacher should challenge children to expand ideas, clarify misunderstandings, and interpret the meaning of their stories. Through these experiences, children will be introduced gradually to the challenging process of revising their writing. They will begin to see that writing is fluid, changing as questions are answered and new ideas are added to it. Children will eventually see the real need for revising their own stories—to make them better and to help the reader understand the exact meaning they are trying to convey.

Introducing the process of revision in a group setting is beneficial in several ways. First, the focus is taken off individual children as the teacher questions and asks for clarification from the entire group. Second, the children themselves are asking questions and making judgments about the story as their peers' ideas are contributed. Finally, as children see the evolution and improvement in pieces that go through the revision process, they will be motivated to revise their own individual writing as opposed to sticking with one-step publishing. One strategy that capitalizes on the social nature of children as they work together in a group to share and negotiate ideas is called cooperative chronicles. While scaffolding plays a major role in all the strategies recommended throughout this book, the cooperative chronicles strategy is explicitly dependent on it.

In writing cooperative chronicles, the teacher scaffolds children's construction of a text from prewriting to publication. The teacher assists with revisions so children see that writing is messy and that stories are revisited and changed to make them better. As this process occurs, the need for creating multiple drafts is realized. This may first be done by using different color markers and creating a legend so children can track the changes. For example, the first draft might be written in black ink, and the first set of subsequent changes made in red, while later changes are made in green. Once a draft becomes filled with changes, children will see the need for it to be rewritten in order to read it clearly. As the draft is copied onto a new page, it is dated; the original draft is kept so it can be compared later to the final published piece. By writing cooperative chronicles, children come to understand in a concrete way that there is more to writing than one-step publishing. They learn through their own actions how a final, polished piece of writing is produced.

■ Origins of Peer Group Writing Strategies

Just as we might research our family trees to learn about our own heritage, tracing contemporary teaching practices to their origin gives us a better appreciation of these practices. We learn how they came to be and why they have persisted or resurfaced over generations. In order to fully understand the cooperative chronicles strategy and its value in introducing children to the process of revising, it might be interesting to be familiar with its origin and lineage. Our cooperative chronicles strategy evolves from the pioneering work in the 1930s of Australian educator Sylvia Ashton-Warner. She is known for devising teaching techniques to reach impoverished Maori children living in a remote area of New Zealand. Ashton-Warner soon realized, as many of us do, that the practices learned in her teacher training were ineffective with the population of children she was hired to teach. After struggling, Ashton-Warner abandoned these traditional methods and, through close observation of her pupils, devised completely new methods that put children and their day-to-day experiences at the center of the learning process. Ashton-Warner quickly discovered that when children are personally involved in writing meaningful text they can read their own stories successfully. As a result, her students became fluent readers and writers and, just as important, felt competent and successful in their ability to do both.

The Language Experience Approach

As educators began experimenting with ways to apply Ashton-Warner's approaches (1963) to teaching techniques in U.S. classrooms (Allen 1976; Hall 1976; Stauffer 1970; Veatch, Sawicki, Elliot, Barnett, and Blackey 1973), the Language Experience Approach (LEA) emerged and has been widely used ever since. LEA involves children in talking and writing about an experience as a group. The following framework provides a premise for understanding LEA:

- What I think is important.

- What I think, I can say.

- What I say can be written down by me or by others.

- What is written down can be read by me and by others. (Morrow 2005b, p. 128)

The first step is to provide a novel stimulus that the children share. Often, teachers and children write an LEA story after going on a field trip or participating in a special event at the school. Books can also be a stimulus for an LEA as well as unexpected occurrences throughout the day. (In my first grade classroom, my students and I shared the experience of a small, brown mouse scampering across the floor, which served as a perfect topic for writing.) After a topic has been selected, a general discussion about the experience can get the ideas flowing. Through discussions, children organize their thoughts and think about the experience from beginning to end.

Next, the teacher writes down on chart paper the children's oral contributions to the story while modeling neat handwriting and correct spelling. The children's words, however, are written as dictated, including grammatical inconsistencies, poor word choices, and events out of sequence. Preserving children's language is a significant characteristic of LEA. "It is a great temptation to change the child's language to the teacher's own, in either word choice or grammar, but editing should be kept to a minimum so that children do not get the impression that their language is inferior or inadequate" (Tompkins 2004, p. 32).

The final step of LEA is to read the text aloud with the children and make it available to students by placing the chart in a designated area of the classroom where children can go to read it on their own. Children can also be provided with an individual copy to read in groups or to take home to share. The teacher may extend the experience further by having children illustrate the text.

Emergence of Shared Writing and Interactive Writing

After decades of using the Language Experience Approach in classrooms, educators began incorporating contemporary research findings on children's writing into this tried and true approach. Inspired by Don Holdaway's (1979) ideas on shared reading experiences with big books, Moira McKenzie (1985) devised a "shared writing" approach, which placed a great emphasis on planning before writing and making appropriate word choices in order to create a text that children can read later. Inspired by McKenzie's shared writing approach, teachers began experimenting with *how* a text is constructed and increased the level of children's involvement in creating text. The result was the "interactive writing" approach in which children not only contribute to the content but actually do the writing, or "share the pen," with the teacher during strategic points of constructing the text. Children are called on to write letters, letter clusters, and familiar words, as they use spacing and punctuation (McCarrier, Pinnell, and Fountas 2000; Tompkins 2004).

Figure 6–1 *A comparison of peer group writing strategies.*

Interactive Writing	Cooperative Chronicles
Children take turns writing	Teacher does the actual writing
Teacher determines sequence of story and much of content	Children choose complete content of story
Great emphasis on counting how many words and letters as well as grapheme-phoneme relationships	Children revisit story to revise for sequence, content, and word choice
Follow-up activities are conducted to reinforce skills	Completed stories are published and shared with others
Stories are for the children's use; not typically shared with others	Several stories may be started but not all completed through publication

Emergence of Cooperative Chronicles

Cooperative chronicles provides yet another valuable strategy derived from the LEA for scaffolding children's writing. Returning to our family lineage analogy, cooperative chronicles is a distant cousin to shared writing and interactive writing. It is different from interactive writing experiences that emphasize phonics and specific skills. Instead, cooperative chronicles maintains a focus on creating meaningful text and introducing children to the process of revising their writing. See Figure 6–1 for a comparison of group peer writing strategies.

■ Cooperative Chronicles: How-To

The first step of writing a cooperative chronicle is determining the topic of the text and deciding on the form of the final published product. Like creating an LEA, it is important that the children write about an experience they have shared and can relate to. Typically, ideas for a topic are generated from class discussions followed by negotiations as final decisions are made. The other significant aspect of planning is deciding on the final format of the published piece. Teachers could make it known that there will be a published product at the end of the process and negotiate with children as they offer possible suggestions for publishing. For example, children may choose to write a narrative account about a class field trip to pick blackberries. As the discussion progresses, it might be decided that, instead of writing a narrative, they will publish a letter thanking the property owner for inviting them to visit.

After these decisions are made in the planning phase, the teacher initiates an open discussion about the experience, and children brainstorm highlights that may be included. The teacher then serves as scribe, writing on chart paper or an overhead projector as children dictate their interpretation of the experience. As in the LEA, the teacher writes the children's contributions in the order they are offered and just as they are stated, without imposing corrections. As she writes, the teacher skips lines or leaves space between lines of written text so that revisions can be made later.

Revising

The distinctive feature of cooperative chronicles is revising the piece to improve the clarity of the text and the quality of the writing. After the first draft is completed, the children suspend work and move to another activity. After a few hours or within one or two days, the draft is revisited to make changes and improvements through revising. Revisions are made with a different color of pen or marker to indicate changes. The teacher and children read the text aloud together and then consider ways to improve what has been written. The teacher can suggest a focus for revising by introducing three distinct elements of the text: sequence, content, and descriptive vocabulary. Depending on the age and ability of the authors, the text may be revised more than once, focusing on one element at a time.

SEQUENCE

During the first draft, young children initially share aspects of their experience without regard to the sequence of events. As the teacher reads the first draft aloud, children listen to determine if the events are in the correct order. If they discover a discrepancy, the teacher simply circles the sentence and draws an arrow to the appropriate section; with older children, the teacher may use a numbering system to indicate the order in which sentences will be written in the published piece.

CONTENT

As the teacher reads the first draft aloud, the children listen to make sure the content is accurate and that it expresses what the writers wanted to say. This step also ensures that important aspects of the experience haven't been left out.

DESCRIPTIVE VOCABULARY

While listening to the teacher reading the first draft aloud, the children think about changing specific words used to make the piece sound more interesting. This may include adding adjectives and adverbs or substituting nouns and verbs. A thesaurus can be introduced as a way of finding synonyms.

Publishing

As with each strategy described in this book, cooperative chronicles places a strong emphasis on publishing and sharing written work with others. Publishing is the ultimate reason for taking the time and trouble to write. It can take many different forms, including copying the text to chart paper and hanging it on a bulletin board or posting the account on the school's website. Individual copies can be typed, printed, and sent home for each child to read aloud for homework. Visitors may be invited to the classroom, such as the principal or students from another grade level, to listen as children read the finished text as a choral reading. Cooperative chronicles might also be written in the form of letters that are placed in an envelope and mailed.

After children become thoroughly familiar with publishing cooperative chronicles, the teacher can offer the children choices regarding which first drafts of texts will be revised to the point of publication. Experienced writers begin multiple drafts and see only a fraction of these through to publication. Introducing this concept during cooperative chronicles can demonstrate to children that it is acceptable to start a story and then abandon it if they like a new topic better. Cooperative chronicles strategy shows children how much work and effort goes into revising to the point of publication, emphasizing the importance of selecting topics they feel passionate about. The following overview summarizes the cooperative chronicles strategy:

Cooperative Chronicles at-a-Glance

1. Plan by choosing a topic and selecting a format for publishing.
2. Have an oral discussion about the shared experience.
3. Create a first draft (skip lines for editing later). Leave the text and revisit it later.*
4. When text is revisited, revise sequence, content, and descriptive vocabulary.
5. Publish the text. Children read and reread the published piece.

---

* Children may decide *not* to revise a piece after revisiting it.

Types of Writing to Publish as Cooperative Chronicles

Teachers use cooperative chronicles to introduce various forms of writing. Narratives and letters written about shared experiences, forms commonly used in the traditional LEA, are appropriate for cooperative chronicles as well. Other categories of writing that can be introduced through cooperative chronicles include fiction writing, how-to informational reports, and poetry. Descriptions and examples of these types of writing are discussed in further detail in the next sections.

Narratives on Shared Experiences

Narratives are the most common type of writing used in group composition experiences—children write about an experience they have shared and publish it as a story to share or a letter to mail. For example, following a field trip to Krispy Kreme Doughnuts®, kindergarten teacher Lisa engaged her class in writing a story about the experience. She began by having the children tell about the things they remembered, and she recorded their recollections with marker on chart paper. The children shared the events of the day as they came to mind, rather than in chronological order. When Lisa read the story aloud, the children immediately realized that the events were out of order. Lisa used this opportunity to teach the children about the need for revising. In order for the children to revise the story, Lisa cut apart each sentence and the class helped rearrange them on the floor. After several attempts, the children were satisfied that the story was in sequence. Lisa then numbered each sentence and taped them together in order.

Later in the day, Lisa overheard one child say to another, "We forgot to include the part about riding and singing on the bus." She used this comment as a springboard for a second revision. Lisa reread the story aloud and asked the children if there was anything they wanted to change. Changes were made in content and word choice by writing them in with a marker.

The next day, Lisa typed each sentence on a separate page, printed them out, and asked the children to work in pairs to illustrate a page of the story. The children worked as a group to assemble the pages in the correct order, using the numbered chart as their guide. As Lisa reread the finished story, the children decided on a title. A cover was made from tag board, featuring a photo of the class while on the field trip, and the book was bound into a publication. As was the custom with cooperative chronicles written in this class, the children took

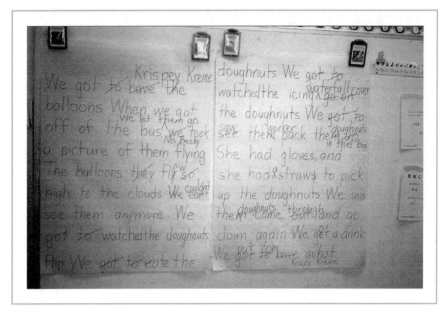

Cooperative chronicle in progress.

turns taking the book home and reading it to their family. (See Appendix B for a letter to parents that accompanies class-made books.) From this experience, the children in Lisa's class learned that stories can be changed after they are written and that the process of publishing requires time and delayed gratification. They also gained a deep satisfaction for producing a piece of writing that was celebrated by their families.

Letters Inspired by Class Content

Letters are an ideal format for a cooperative chronicle. The purpose of the writing is clear: to convey thoughts or feelings to another person. The letter itself, therefore, becomes a published piece because it is shared with another. Classes can write letters to practically anyone, including school personnel, parent volunteers, politicians, famous people, and children's book authors and illustrators. Using the cooperative chronicle strategy, teachers introduce the format of writing a letter. Letters written on large chart paper can be sent in that form in a large envelope or they can be rewritten or typed on school stationery. Some letters may be written on postcards or sent as an email. For example, the following cooperative chronicle was written as part of a science unit.

Kelly and her second-grade students were studying whales as part of a science unit on mammals. After reading about Shamu, the famous killer whale at

SeaWorld®, and using the SeaWorld® website as a resource for facts and photographs, the children had questions about the whale's care and training. Kelly noticed an email address and suggested that they compose a letter to send. The class began working on the letter immediately using the cooperative chronicle strategy. Kelly wrote the children's questions and ideas for the email on the computer, which was projected on a television so all could see it. The children asked: "What does Shamu eat?" "How much does Shamu eat in a day?" "How long does it take to teach a new trick?" and numerous other questions. When they finished the draft, Kelly recommended that they revise their email after lunch before sending it. The children had wanted to send it immediately, but after revisiting the letter that afternoon, they realized some changes needed to be made. One of their questions was already answered on the website. Other questions were too similar to each other, so these were revised. They changed the word *trick* to *behavior* after reading more about training on the website. While revising, they decided to add two sentences about how exciting it must be to work with killer whales. When the letter was complete, Kelly and her students read it aloud one last time before she sent the email. She also printed out a copy to put on the science bulletin board. All that afternoon, Kelly's students pestered her to check for a reply. After only a couple of hours, they received an email from Shamu's trainers. The children were so excited they decided to make individual birthday cards for Shamu to send to the trainers.

These second-graders experienced firsthand the power of writing. Using technology enabled them to get a quick reply to their email, which was a great motivator since so much of writing involves delayed gratification. They also saw the benefits of mastering keyboarding skills, which eventually becomes a necessary skill for fluent writers.

Fiction Writing

In fiction writing, the characteristics of a particular genre of story, such as folklore, fantasy, or realistic fiction, are used to write a new story. Children become familiar with the characteristics through their exposure to classic and contemporary fiction. A practical way to approach fictional writing through cooperative chronicles is by retelling familiar stories.

RETELLINGS

Retellings involve children in reconstructing a story with which they are familiar. Children demonstrate their deep understanding of the plot and characters as they recall the story in a retelling. A cooperative chronicle can be written after reading a book to children two or three times so they are thoroughly familiar with the story. Or, the teacher might choose to immerse children in more than one version of the same classic tale. The class may participate in Readers' Theater in which the teacher serves as narrator reading central parts of the story while the children take on the roles of different characters, reading their lines from the story.

Ashley introduced her kindergarten class to Steven Kellogg's *The Three Little Pigs* (2002). The children enjoyed the book and regularly asked her to read it again. After becoming familiar with the text, Ashley suggested the class perform a Readers' Theater. The children took turns playing the roles of the pigs, the wolf, and the straw, wood, and brick salesmen. Now very familiar with the story, the class wrote their own retelling, which was later revised to add more conversation between the characters. The story was published by posting the final revision written on chart paper outside the classroom door. The children's art and digital photographs from their Readers' Theater highlighted the publication.

Down the hall, second-graders were also reading about the three pigs. In this class, however, they were reading *The True Story of the Three Little Pigs* by Jon Scieszka (1996). This version tells the story from the point of view of the wolf. As second-graders, these children have moved beyond the egocentric thought that dominates the thinking of younger children and can shift their thinking to accommodate another's perspective. Delighted by the wolf's whimsical excuses for his bad behavior, they asked for more stories written in this style. The teacher treated her students to a series of flip books published by Steck-Vaughn that tell familiar stories from two different perspectives including *Rumpelstiltskin/A Deal Is a Deal* (Granowsky et al. 1993), *Peter Pan/Grow up, Peter Pan!* (Barrie et al. 1994), and *Robin Hood/The Sheriff Speaks* (Granowsky et al. 1993). She also added to the class library the following titles. *Goldilocks and the Three Bears/Bears Should Share!* (Granowsky et al. 1996), *Jack and the Beanstalk/Giants Have Feelings, Too* (Granowsky et al. 1996), and *Three Billy Goats Gruff: Just a Friendly Old Troll* (Granowsky et al. 1996).

The teacher suggested the class write a cooperative chronicle in which a well-known storybook villain defends his or her actions. After brainstorming several titles and scenarios, the students decided to write a retelling of the story of "Goldilocks and the Three Bears" from the point of view of a naughty little girl who proclaims her innocence. After final revisions were made, the story was copied into a book made by stapling paper between cardstock front and back covers. The children worked in pairs to complete the illustrations. Children took turns checking the book out from the classroom library to take it home and share it with their families.

Informational Reports

Using cooperative chronicles to write informational reports is ideal for integrating writing into other content areas, especially social studies or science. Teachers can introduce children to this genre of writing through high-quality children's books written on topics of interest to young children. The Internet can also be used to access facts to include in informational reports. Young children's first informational reports easily can be written in the form of "All About…" books in which a single fact about a subject they have studied is written on each page of a book and then illustrated (Tompkins 2005). For example, after the school nurse visited and conducted a demonstration, Lucy's first-grade class wrote an informational report listing the steps for hand washing. After revising, the text was written on chart paper and given to the nurse to hang in the first-aid room.

Second- and third-graders can conduct research on a topic, such as dinosaurs, in small groups and then come together to report their findings by writing a cooperative chronicle. Writing informational reports in this way gives teachers a great opportunity to model for children how to paraphrase information. Children can learn the concept of plagiarism, why it is wrong, and how it can be avoided. This exercise reduces the risk of children copying facts out of a book when they begin writing reports independently. Cooperatives chronicles written as informational reports can be published in book form and, after the class has moved on to another topic of study, can be donated to the school library as reference material.

Poetry

As children master oral language, they begin to play with words by making up silly songs and nonsense words or by using sound effects to emphasize a point. Their interest in poetry grows as they sing familiar tunes, repeat nursery rhymes, attempt tongue twisters, or read from a memorized Dr. Seuss book. Writing poetry can evolve naturally from these early playful experiences with words and sounds. Writing poetry together as a group gives children the support they need when learning to write in a new genre and is fun for children as they share ideas. Formula poems work particularly well when written as cooperative chronicles.

FORMULA POEMS

Formula poems use repetition, as opposed to rhyme, for a poetic device, making it easier for children to compose original poetry. A basic frame or pattern is provided for writing formula poems, yet they are very flexible and provide much room for variation and creativity. Three types of formula poems recommended by Kenneth Koch, poet and author of *Wishes, Lies, and Dreams* (2000), include color poems, "If I Were..., Then I Would..." poems, and "I Wish..." poems.

COLOR POEMS

Prekindergarten and kindergarten children can apply their knowledge of color names and their ability to identify the color of objects as they write a color poem by naming and describing a color for each line. They may think of multiple descriptions for a single color or choose different colors. Color poems can be published by writing them on an overhead transparency, using the corresponding color of marker for each line. For a follow-up activity, the teacher can project the poem onto the board and ask the children to circle the color words using the corresponding dry-erase markers.

"IF I WERE..., THEN I WOULD..." POEMS

As children describe what it would be like to be a specific person or object, "If I Were..., Then I Would..." formula poems can be written as cooperative chronicles. Each student can contribute to a line of the poem, or the children may bounce ideas off each other and compose the poem with group input. These poems can be tied into thematic units of study.

"I WISH..." POEMS

A third formula poem begins with the line, "I wish..." and children simply fill in a wish. This format can be done using random wishes, or the children can write a poem in response to an event that holds meaning for them.

Encouraging
Independent Authors

Writing and Publishing on Their Own

7

If you wish to be a writer, write.

—Epictetus

Whether we are holding a toddler's hands as he takes his first wobbly steps or biting our tongue as a teenage driver slams on the brakes, the goal that we strive for is the same: one day he will be able to walk around the house unassisted and she will be able to drive alone safely and confidently. Independence is also our ultimate goal in those we teach. Children move along the literacy continuum, beginning with complete dependence on another to write down their stories, then applying new skills and strategies with support from others, until finally reaching the point where they are capable of communicating in writing independent of continual help from others. At this point children become independent authors.

Those capable of independent authorship possess many literacy skills that others do not. They have learned to distinguish print from picture and writing from non-writing. They have acquired phonemic awareness—a major milestone of literacy development. They have also become increasingly dissatisfied with invented spellings, and as a result, they are more conscious of spelling patterns, sight words, print from their environment, and sources of help for spelling words conventionally, such as asking peers, picking up the dictionary, or using the spell-check function on the word processor. Independent authors are more confident in their ability to select their topics, clarify their meaning through revisions, and share their finished product with others. As with other areas of development, time and maturation changes the way children read and write (Teale and Sulzby 1986).

Our role as teachers also transforms once children are capable of writing independent of direct assistance. We change from enabler to facilitator. Once we were the means for children to get their ideas on paper; now they are cognitively and physically capable of doing that on their own. Instead of being directly involved in putting stories in print, teachers are available to serve as coach and motivator (Fletcher and Portalupi 2001) as children create independent products. In this role, we sustain children's motivation to write by providing an organizational strategy for daily writing (writing workshop), a designated space with useful tools and materials for writing and publishing (publishing center), and new purposes for writing (integrated curriculum).

◼ Writing Workshop

First and foremost, teachers facilitate children's writing by establishing a routine for writing, a plan for providing relevant instruction, and an organizational system for keeping track of story ideas, drafts, multiple revisions, and published pieces. Writing workshop, a system widely recognized for its success in developing lifelong writers, incorporates the five-part cycle of the writing process, including prewriting, drafting, revising, editing, and publishing. As children told their stories orally, they were engaged in *prewriting*. Kid writing was used to *draft*, or put thoughts down on paper, which was translated to conventional spelling as needed. When children contributed ideas as a group, they were introduced to the need for *revision* and *editing*. And they saw firsthand that *publishing*, and sharing their stories, is the primary purpose for writing.

Donald Graves, a pioneer in research on teaching writing, is credited with recognizing the competence of children as authors of topics that are personally meaningful. In his now classic book, *Writing: Teachers and Children at Work* (2003), Graves shows us what children can do when they receive support (rather than interference) from adults who recognize their ability as writers. Since this pivotal publication, other researchers have contributed to our understanding of how to approach the teaching of writing from Graves' perspective. It is from this body of research that the writing workshop emerged as a tried-and-true method for teaching children the joy of writing (Calkins 1994; Fletcher and Portalupi 2001; Ray 2004; Solley 2005).

As with most highly effective teaching strategies, there is no one correct way to conduct writing workshop. No exact amount of time must be established for all teachers to follow and no written script provided from which teachers must read. Instead, the guidelines for holding a writing workshop are dependent on the learners and their needs. For example, kindergarten children may need more time to physically move within the classroom space and get materials ready but will spend less time engaged with pencil to paper than second-graders. Developmental variables must be considered when making schedules, and teachers need to be flexible in making accommodations as needed.

However, three basic considerations must be addressed when making decisions regarding when and how children will participate in writing workshop. The first is how space will be arranged, already addressed in Chapter 3. The second is how to use writing folders as a way to organize materials. The third is how to manage time.

Writing Folders

Children can be given individual two-pocket folders that will serve as organizational containers to hold their works in progress. Among the items included in the folder can be an ongoing list of possible topics children may want to write about in the future. Children should be encouraged to think of themselves as writers by making notes of possible topics for stories as they come to mind. Children can keep observation pads, which are a convenient tool for collecting ideas for future stories (Avery 1998). As they come across situations or events that spark an idea for a possible story, children can jot down their observations and ideas. When searching for a topic during writing workshop, children can simply refer back to their observation pad for a myriad of ideas. Observation pads can be made by stapling together large blank index cards on which children can draw a sketch and give it a title, or simply write down a few words to remind them of their idea for a story. Small notebooks can be used in the same way.

Through writing workshop, children can work over a period of time on drafts of stories in their writing folders, applying writing skills they have learned such as revising and editing. After completing the first draft of a story, they can return to it another day to make revisions. Before publishing their story, children edit their work with the help of their peers and the teacher. The degree to which the piece is edited will depend on the child and her abilities. While teachers encourage children to use language arts skills and spelling strategies when they edit, they do not expect the piece to be completely polished with no errors. For example, children may publish pieces that include some forms of kid writing, such as invented spelling, but they are encouraged to use available reference materials. Children can use a word wall of correctly spelled words from their spelling units or resources that are kept in their writing folder, such as a list of sight words for their grade level or a personal dictionary.

Personal dictionaries, teacher-made booklets with separate blank pages for each letter of the alphabet, help children learn to spell words conventionally in their writing. When children edit their writing prior to publication or come across a word they want to learn how to spell, they add it to the corresponding-letter page in their personal dictionary. Younger children can draw a picture to help them remember the word, but the timing of when to introduce personal dictionaries is critical. It is best to wait until children are confident in their ability as inventive spellers. If this tool is introduced too early, it could send the message that it is always necessary to spell correctly, hindering a child's invented spelling. If introduced before a child is comfortable with inventing spellings, the personal dictionary can become an additional roadblock for those who already refuse to take risks in their writing. Once the personal dictionary is introduced, teachers must be observant to ensure that children do not revert back to selecting only words they can spell correctly.

A final item to be included in the writing folder is a writing log that can be as simple or complex as the teacher chooses to make it. (See Appendix C for a sample of a writing log.) The writing log serves as a chronological record for each story started and can include a space to indicate the parts of the writing

An entry is made in the log that is kept in the writing folder.

process used and the stories that made it through to publication. As the writing folder and its contents become a part of the daily routine, the children's writing behavior will mimic that of accomplished writers, and they will develop the persistence and determination to see a piece of writing through to publication.

Managing Time

The block of time designated for writing workshop can be broken down into three components: instructional time in which the teacher introduces a specific skill or strategy that can be incorporated into children's writing, writing time in which children are engaged in uninterrupted writing, and share time in which children are allowed to give and receive feedback about their writing. Although the schedule and amount of time dedicated to these three components of writing workshop can vary, a one-hour writing workshop can be broken down as follows: a five- to ten-minute minilesson, thirty-five to forty-five minutes for writing, and ten to twenty minutes for share time (Fletcher and Portalupi 2001). It may be difficult, however, to keep young children involved in a single writing activity for the suggested thirty-five- to forty-five-minute period. Therefore, we recommend a developmentally appropriate routine in which children choose from a variety of activities (such as those suggested in Chapters 2 and 3). It is expected that each child will complete specific activities, such as working on a story in her writing folder, before moving to other activities that have been set up around the classroom in learning centers. Within the thirty-five- to forty-five-minute writing period, a child may revise a story she had previously started in her writing folder, or work in the computer or library center.

A typical question asked by teachers planning their schedule is, "How many days a week do children participate in writing workshop?" Again, this depends on the needs of the learners, but there are guidelines. Fletcher and Portalupi (2001) recommend four or five days a week, with a minimum of three. Donald Graves (2003) warns that not teaching writing at all is preferable to letting children write only occasionally because the infrequent exposure to writing will make it a chore rather than a pleasure. We recommend that once children become independent in their writing they take part in scheduled writing workshop every day they come to school. We feel this is especially important for young children because they need predictable, daily routines to give them a sense of security and confidence. Also, since young children's concept of time is different from adults, a Monday, Wednesday, Friday schedule for writing workshop may make sense to the teacher but seems sporadic and inconsistent to children.

■ Publishing Materials

Independent authors will not produce the volume of published pieces they did when dictating anecdotes or creating cooperative chronicles. Working alone, the independent author identifies the topic and, if he chooses, sees it through to the point of publication. While the ultimate responsibility for the published piece lies with the author, the teacher assists as needed, providing moral support, supplying materials, and offering ideas for traditional and novel ways to publish stories. Through this process, children become aware that it is sharing, rather than simply producing, that actually makes writing a form of communication.

Materials and resources to make available to independent authors in the publishing center include:

- A variety of sizes, colors, shapes, and textures of paper, as well as envelopes, stationery, greeting cards, cardstock, catalogs, magazines, graph paper, and wallpaper samples
- Self-adhesive notes and labels of various sizes, notebooks, adding machine tape, sentence strips, note cards, clipboards, invoices, order forms, and receipt books
- Instruments for writing and drawing including pencils, erasers, pens, colored pencils, crayons, markers, and commercial art supplies designed with young children in mind
- Letter/number stickers, upper/lowercase letter stamps, and ink pads
- Chalkboard and chalk or dry-erase board and markers
- Story response sheets/charts, motivational pictures, and picture albums of past creations/constructions
- Picture dictionary, children's thesaurus, word bank, class list, and synonym/antonym charts
- Materials used to bind pages together such as a long-arm stapler, hole punch, three-ring hole puncher, rings, brads, yarn, string, ribbon, glue, glue sticks, and tape of different widths
- Pre-made books of differing size, shape, and length
- Children's journals
- Computer and publishing software
- Volunteers to assist children with publishing

Madison binds her book using a stapler in the publishing center.

As children become more confident in their abilities as independent authors, they enjoy novel methods for publishing their writing. These methods may include simple pop-up books, flip books, stapleless books, shape books, and books of various sizes (Boardman-Moen 1999; O'Brien-Palmer 2001; Sunflower 1999). A new twist can be added by publishing children's writing using creative fonts or by reducing the font size so small that a magnifiying glass is needed to read it. For significant pieces of children's writing with accompanying illustrations, teachers may choose to have it published in hardback form by a publishing service. Once such company, Studentreasures® (www.studentreasures.com), will publish one book per student at no cost with an option to purchase additional copies. Introducing new methods for publishing keeps children interested and serves as a motivation to write.

Technology

The ever-increasing evolution of technology and software is an invaluable resource to publishing children's writing. Word processing reduces time spent recopying during the revision process (Tompkins 2004) and built-in spelling and grammar tools assist with editing. Children can practice keyboarding skills through entertaining, age-appropriate software. This resource is especially beneficial to children with fine-motor limitations and attention deficits.

Computer programs can be used to produce creative and professional-looking publications. Various versions of The Print Shop® are available that make it possible for children to create newsletters, postcards, signs, certificates, calendars, and greeting cards, or add borders and clipart to their printed text. Kid Pix® Deluxe 4, Home Edition helps children create artwork using a variety of "virtual media." Print options are available for children to customize the text formatting of their stories. Another useful feature is that the program can be run

---

Figure 7–1 *Magazines That Publish Children's Work.*

Online Magazines

www.cyberkids.com
This online magazine for children ages seven to twelve publishes stories, poems, articles, drawings, or other creative work that is original. Funny pieces are preferred; games, puzzles, and brainteasers are also accepted.

www.kidsbookshelf.com
This site publishes children's short stories (500 words maximum), poetry (200 words maximum), reviews of children's books (500 words maximum), and original artwork of children seventeen years and younger.

www.kidpub.org
Publishes children's work on the site as well as provides classroom teachers with a webpage dedicated and accessible only to the students in the class. The teacher is given a password to maintain the site. There is a nominal one-time fee to assist with expenses related to maintaining COPPA records.

www.writingconference.com
East Carolina University publishes children's work from kindergarten through twelfth grade including fiction, nonfiction, artwork, poetry, and plays.

Print Magazines

Kid's World: Morgan Kopaska-Merkel, Editor
1300 Kicker Rd.
Tuscaloosa, AL 35404
Publishes children's (ages two through seventeen years) artwork, comics, jokes, and riddles.

Stone Soup: Gerry Mandel, Articles/Fiction Editor
Children's Art Foundation
P.O. Box 83
Santa Cruz, CA 95063
Publishes fiction and nonfiction, artwork, poetry, and book reviews from children through age thirteen.

---

in English or Spanish, so it provides an instant translation for English language learners and their families.

Photography provides an interesting way for children to personalize their publications. With digital cameras becoming more and more affordable, children can use digital photos that relate to their story or add interest to an "All About the Author" page with a single digital photo of themselves. Digital photos can also be added to "reviews" children give about the books their classmates write. If a digital camera is not available, children can use a scanner to upload photos to the computer.

Internet websites are available for posting children's writing for a wider audience to enjoy. Published pieces can be placed on secure school websites or on school district websites that are accessible through the World Wide Web. The simplified process of publishing print material online has resulted in more magazines that specifically publish children's work. (See Figure 7–1 for a list of these magazines.)

When choosing sites for publishing children's work, parents and teachers need to be familiar with the Children's Online Privacy Protection Act 1998 (COPPA). A number of controls are in place that parents can use to limit the information that can be given about a child. For example, a story may be published giving only the author's first name, last initial, city, and state of residency as opposed to more detailed, private information. The website for the Center for Democracy and Technology (www.cdt.org/legislation) provides the legal ruling of COPPA, but for an easy-to-read interpretation of the law, go to the Kidz Privacy website (www.ftc.gov).

■ Integrated Curriculum

Integrating literacy learning into other curriculum areas provides authentic writing experiences. When children have the opportunity to share what they have learned about a topic of interest with their peers, they are using writing skills in a genuine and meaningful way. They are also using the writing process as they write notes using invented spellings, revise their pieces based on feedback from peers, and publish in a final format.

There are many creative ways for children to publish informational reports on science or social studies topics. After reading *The Best Vacation Ever* (Murphy and Westcott 1997), Kristine and Paige, two second-grade teachers, came up with different ideas for integrating social studies research skills with authentic writing opportunities. Kristine focused on the concept of travel and prepared for the lesson by collecting brochures from local travel agencies. She introduced the brochures to the children, pointing out the beautiful photography and reading excerpts that gave inviting descriptions of exotic destinations. Then she introduced the word *amenities* and listed them as they appeared in the passage. Next, she assigned children the task of making their own travel brochures. They were allowed to choose any destination and use resources available to them such as the brochures from the travel agencies, encyclopedias, and the Internet. Over several days, the children collected and wrote about destinations from Russia to Disney World. Then Kristine invited the children to publish their brochures in booklets she had made by stapling lined handwriting paper into a folded construction-paper cover. The children wrote the name of their destination on the cover and their descriptive passages and list of amenities inside. They glued in photographs downloaded from the Internet and wrote captions. Finally, the children shared their travel brochures by reading them aloud to the class and lining them up on the chalkboard rail for others to view.

Paige took a different approach to the same story. After reading *The Best Vacation Ever*, each child drew a strip of paper from a bowl with the name of a state written on it. Then they checked out a corresponding book from a set of reference materials in the library. The children researched facts about their assigned state, such as state flag, bird, flower, and tree, as well as industry and population statistics. The children included the information they found particularly interesting, such as professional sports teams in the state or famous people born there. They published their findings in accordion-fold books with an outline of the state on the cover and related drawings and photographs on some of the pages. The children shared their books throughout the week and then placed them all in a labeled plastic bin in the class library. Both Kristine and Paige recognized the importance of celebrating independent authors and their accomplishments.

Children's accomplishments as writers should be celebrated at every step of the way. From the time when they are able to tell their stories only orally until they publish a piece independently, their efforts, struggles, and successes should each be recognized as part of the journey of becoming a writer. As teachers, our job is much more than teaching the skills and strategies for composing a complete passage. It is our responsibility to instill in children a love for the craft of writing and for sharing their thoughts, ideas, and beliefs with others through the written word. It is never too soon to kindle a passion for writing in children, so…get them writing now!

Appendix A

Record of Center Use

Date: _____

Children's Names																					
Art Center																					
Library/Listening Center																					
Block Center																					
Computer Center																					
Discovery Center																					
Dramatic Play Center																					
Fine Motor Center																					
Math Center																					
Publishing Center																					

Appendix B

Dear Parents,

We will be making many class books during the year. These books are written by the class as a whole group or each child contributes to the book as an individual. We read our self-published books repeatedly in class, and then they are sent home to be shared before placing them in our class library. Today, your child is bringing home a book he or she helped write to share with your family. Please take some time to read this book aloud with your child. You may add your own thoughts about their accomplishment on the last page labeled, "Book Reviews." Then, send the book back tomorrow so another child can take it home.

Please remember to recognize your child for his or her effort as a published writer!

Appendix C

Writing Log

DATE:	TITLE:	PROGRESS: (circle)
		PRE DRAFT RVS ED PUB
		PRE DRAFT RVS ED PUB
		PRE DRAFT RVS ED PUB
		PRE DRAFT RVS ED PUB
		PRE DRAFT RVS ED PUB
		PRE DRAFT RVS ED PUB
		PRE DRAFT RVS ED PUB
		PRE DRAFT RVS ED PUB
		PRE DRAFT RVS ED PUB

Name:_____

References

ALLEN, R. V. 1976. *Language Experience in Communication*. Boston: Houghton Mifflin.

ASHTON-WARNER, S. 1963. *Teacher*. New York: Simon & Schuster.

AVERY, N. 1998. "Using Observation Pads as a Prewriting Tool." *Teaching K–8* (September).

AYELSWORTH, J. and MCCLINTOCK, B. 1998. *The Gingerbread Man*. New York: Scholastic.

BARRIE, J. M., GRANOWSKY, A., MARCHESI, S., CHENG, J., and CHILDRESS, R. 1994. *Peter Pan/Grow up, Peter Pan!* New York: Steck-Vaughn.

BEATTY, J. 2006. *Observing Development of the Young Child*. Sixth Edition. Upper Saddle River, NJ: Pearson/Merrill Prentice Hall.

BERK, L. E. 2002. *Child Development*. Sixth Edition. Boston: Allyn and Bacon.

BISSEX, G. L. 1980. *Gnys at Wrk: A Child Learns to Write and Read*. Cambridge, MA: Harvard University Press.

BLOOM, B. S. 1969. *Taxonomy of Educational Objectives: The Classification of Educational Goals Handbook*. New York: D. McKay/Longman.

BOARDMAN-MOEN, C. 1999. *Better than Book Reports: More than Forty Creative Responses to Literature (Grades 2–6)*. New York: Scholastic.

BROWN, G. H. 1977. "Development of Story in Children's Reading and Writing." *Theory Into Practice 16*(5), 357–62.

BRUNER, J. 1992. *Acts of Meaning*. Cambridge, MA: Harvard University Press.

CALKINS, L. 1994. *The Art of Teaching Writing*. Portsmouth, NH: Heinemann.

CAMBOURNE, B. 1987. "Language, Learning, and Literacy." In Butler, A. and Turnbill, J., eds., *Towards a Reading-Writing Classroom* (pp. 5–10). Portsmouth, NH: Heinemann.

CHOMSKY, N. 1965. *Aspects of a Theory of Syntax*. Cambridge, MA: MIT Press.

CLAY, M. 1975. *What Did I Write?* Portsmouth, NH: Heinemann.

CLAY, M. 1979. *The Early Detection of Reading Difficulties: A Diagnostic Survey with Recovery Procedures*. Auckland, New Zealand: Heinemann Educational Books.

CLAY, M. 1991. *Becoming Literate: The Construction of Inner Control.* Portsmouth, NH: Heinemann.

CUMMINS, J. 1979. "Linguistic Interdependence and the Educational Development of Bilingual Children." *Review of Educational Research 49*: 222–251.

DE TEMPLE, J. M. and TABORS, P. O. 1996. "Children's Story Retelling as a Predictor of Early Reading Achievement." Paper presented at the Biennial Meeting of the International Society for the Study of Behavioral Development. Quebec City, Quebec. ERIC Document Reproduction No. 403 543.

DORROS, A. and KLEVEN, E. 1997. *Abuela.* New York: Puffin Books.

DUKE, N. K. and KAYS, J. 1998. "'Can I Say "Once Upon a Time"?': Kindergarten Children's Developing Knowledge of Information Book Language." *Early Childhood Research Quarterly 13,* 295–318.

DUKE, N. K. and PURCELL-GATES, V. 2003. "Genres at Home and at School: Bridging the Known to the New." *The Reading Teacher 57,* 30–37.

FEELINGS, M. and FEELINGS, T. 1992. *Jambo Means Hello: Swahili Alphabet Book.* New York: Puffin Books.

FLETCHER, R. and PORTALUPI, J. 2001. *Writing Workshop: The Essential Guide.* Portsmouth, NH: Heinemann.

GENTILE, L. M. and HOOT, J. L. 1983. "Kindergarten Play: The Foundation of Reading." *The Reading Teacher 36,* 436–39.

GRANOWSKY, A., BUERCHKHOLTZ, H., and GRAVES, L. D. 1996. *Jack and the Beanstalk/Giants Have Feelings, Too.* New York: Steck-Vaughn.

GRANOWSKY, A., GRIFFIN, D., and FITZHUGH, G. 1993. *Robin Hood/The Sheriff Speaks.* New York: Steck-Vaughn.

GRANOWSKY, A., LUNSFORD, A., and MARTIN, L. 1996. *Goldilocks and the Three Bears/Bears Should Share!* New York: Steck-Vaughn.

GRANOWSKY, A., NEWBURY, T., and GRAVES, L. D. 1993. *A Deal Is a Deal/Rumpelstiltskin.* New York: Steck-Vaughn.

GRANOWSKY, A., NIDENOFF, M., and NEWBURY, T. 1996. *Three Billy Goats Gruff: Just a Friendly Old Troll.* New York: Steck-Vaughn.

GRAVES, D. 2003. *Writing: Teachers and Children at Work, 20th Anniversary Edition.* Portsmouth, NH: Heinemann.

GUNNING, T. G. 2004. *Creating Literacy Instruction for All Children in Pre-K to 4.* Boston: Allyn and Bacon.

HALL, M. A. 1976. *Teaching Reading as a Language Experience.* Columbus, OH: Merrill.

HANNON, J. 1999. "Talking Back: Kindergarten Dialogue Journals." *The Reading Teacher 53,* 200–03.

HARSTE, J., WOODWARD, V., and BURKE, C. 1984. *Language Stories and Literacy Lessons.* Portsmouth, NH: Heinemann.

HAYES, A. 1990. "From Scribbling to Writing: Smoothing the Way." *Young Children 45*(3), 62–68.

HELLER, M. 1995. *Reading-Writing Connections.* Second Edition. White Plains, NY: Longman.

HILLIKER, J. 1988. "Labeling to Beginning Narrative: Four Kindergarten Children Learn to Write." In Newkirk, T. and Atwell, N., eds., *Understanding Writing*. Second Edition. Portsmouth, NH: Heinemann.

HOLDAWAY, D. 1979. *The Foundations of Literacy*. Portsmouth, NH: Heinemann.

HOPKINSON, D. 1995. *Sweet Clara and the Freedom Quilt*. New York: Dragonfly Books.

IRWIN, P. A. and MITCHELL, J. N. 1983. "A Procedure for Assessing the Richness of Retellings." *Journal of Reading 26*, 391–96.

KASZA, K. 2003. *My Lucky Day*. New York: Penguin Putnam Books for Young Readers.

KELLOGG, S. 2002. *The Three Little Pigs*. New York: HarperCollins.

KIEFF, J. E. and CASBERGUE, R. M. 2000. *Playful Learning and Teaching: Integrating Play into Preschool and Primary Programs*. Boston: Allyn and Bacon.

KLEIN, M., COOK, R., and RICHARDSON-GIBBS, A. 2001. *Strategies for Including Children with Special Needs in Early Childhood Settings*. Albany, NY: Delmar Thomson Learning.

KOCH, K. 1990. *Rose, Where Did You Get That Red?* New York: Vintage.

KOCH, K. 2000. *Wishes, Lies, and Dreams*. New York: HarperPerennial.

LOBEL, A. 1983. *Fables*. New York: HarperTrophy.

MARTINEZ, M., ROSER, N. L., and STRECKER, S. 1999. "'I Never Thought I Could Be a Star': A Readers Theater Ticket to Fluency." *Reading Teacher 52*(4), 326–34.

McCARRIER, A., PINNELL, G., and FOUNTAS, I. 2000. *Interactive Writing: How Language and Literacy Come Together*. Portsmouth, NH: Heinemann.

McGEE, L., LOMAX, R., and HEAD, M. 1988. "Young Children's Written Language Knowledge: What Environmental and Functional Print Reading Reveals." *Journal of Reading Behavior 20*, 99–118.

McKENZIE, M. G. 1985. *Shared Writing: Apprenticeship in Writing in Language Matters*. London: Centre for Language in Primary Education.

MERRITT, D. D. and LILES, B. Z. 1989. "Narrative Analysis: Clinical Applications of Story Generation and Story Retelling." *Journal of Speech and Hearing Disorders 54*, 429–38.

MORRISON, G. S. and RUSHER, A. S. 1999. "Playing to Learn." *Dimensions of Early Childhood 27*(2), 3–8.

MORROW, L. M. 1985. "Retelling Stories: A Strategy for Improving Young Children's Comprehension, Concept of Story Structure, and Oral Language Complexity." *The Elementary School Journal 85*, 647–61.

MORROW, L. M. 1986. "Effects of Structural Guidance in Story Retelling on Children's Dictation of Original Stories." *Journal of Reading Behavior 18*, 135–52.

MORROW, L. M. 1990. "Preparing the Classroom Environment to Promote Literacy During Play." *Early Childhood Research Quarterly 5*, 537–54.

MORROW, L. M. 1996. "Story Retelling: A Discussion Strategy to Develop and Assess Comprehension." In Gambrell, L. and Almasi, J., eds., *Lively Discussions! Fostering Engaged Reading* (pp. 265–85). Newark, DE: International Reading Association.

MORROW, L. M. 2000. *Literacy Development in the Early Years: Helping Children Read and Write*. Fourth Edition. Boston: Allyn & Bacon.

MORROW, L. M. 2005a. "Language and Literacy in Preschools: Current Issues and Concerns." *Literacy Teaching and Learning: An International Journal of Early Reading and Writing 9*(1), 7–19.

MORROW, L. M. 2005b. *Literacy Development in the Early Years: Helping Children Read and Write*. Fifth Edition. Boston: Pearson/Allyn & Bacon.

MURPHY, S. and WESTCOTT, N. 1997. *The Best Vacation Ever*. New York: HarperCollins Children's Books.

NCELA/National Clearinghouse for English Language Acquisition & Language Instruction Educational Programs. 2003. Washington, DC.

NELSON, O. 1989. "Storytelling: Language Experience for Meaning Making." *The Reading Teacher 42*(6), 386–90.

NEUMAN, S. B. and ROSKOS, K. 1990. "Play, Print, and Purpose: Enriching Play Environments for Literacy Development." *The Reading Teacher 44*(3), 214–21.

NEUMAN, S. B. and ROSKOS, K. 1993. "Access to Print for Children of Poverty: Differential Effects of Adult Mediation and Literacy-Enriched Play Settings on Environmental and Functional Print Tasks." *American Educational Research Journal 30*, 95–122.

NEUMAN, S. B. and ROSKOS, K. 1997. "Literacy Knowledge in Practice: Contexts of Participation for Young Writers and Readers." *Reading Research Quarterly 32*, 10–32.

NOUROT, P. M. and VAN HOORN, J. L. 1991. "Symbolic Play in Preschool and Primary Settings." *Young Children 54*, 40–47.

NUMEROFF, L. J. and BOND, F. 1985. *If You Give a Mouse a Cookie*. New York: Laura Geringer.

O'BRIEN-PALMER, M. 2001. *Poetry Pizazz!: 15 Easy, Hands-on Poetry Activities that Invite Kids to Write and Publish Their Poems in Unique and Dazzling Ways*. New York: Scholastic.

OKEN-WRIGHT, P. 1999. "Transition to Writing: Drawing as a Scaffold for Emergent Writers." *Young Children 53*(2), 76–81.

PELLEGRINI, A. D. and GALDA, L. 1982. "The Effects of Thematic-Fantasy Play Training on the Development of Children's Story Comprehension." *American Educational Research Journal 19*, 443–52.

PIAGET, J. 1962. *Play, Dreams, and Imitation in Childhood*. New York: W. W. Norton.

PIAGET, J. 1975. *The Development of Thought: Equilibration of Cognitive Structures*. New York: Viking.

PIAGET, J. 1983. "Piaget's Theory." In W. Kessen, ed., and P. H. Mussen, series ed., *Handbook of Child Psychology: Vol. 1, History, Theory, and Methods* (pp. 103–26). New York: Wiley.

RAY, K. W. 2004. *About the Authors: Writing Workshop with Our Youngest Writers*. Portsmouth, NH: Heinemann.

RITCHIE, S., JAMES-SZANTON, J., and HOWES, C. 2003. "Emergent Literacy Practices in Early Childhood Classrooms." In C. Howes, ed., *Teaching 4- to 8-Year-Olds: Literacy, Math, Multiculturism, and Classroom Community*. (71–92). Baltimore: Brookes.

RONEY, C. R. 1989. "Back to the Basics with Storytelling." *The Reading Teacher 42*(7), 520–23.

ROSKOS, K. A., CHRISTIE, J. F., and RIGELS, D. J. 2003. "The Essentials of Literacy Instruction." *Young Children 58*(2), 52–62.

ROSKOS, K. A., VUKELICH, C., CHRISTIE, J. F., ENZ, B., and NEUMAN, S. B. 1995. *Linking Literacy and Play*. Newark, DE: International Reading Association.

ROUTMAN, R. 1991. *Transitions: From Literature to Literacy*. Portsmouth, NH: Heinemann.

RYLANT, C. 1993. *When I Was Young in the Mountains*. New York: Puffin Books.

SCHICKEDANZ, J. 1982. "The Acquisition of Written Language in Young Children." In B. Spodek, ed., *Handbook of Research in Early Childhood Education*. New York: The Free Press.

SCHICKEDANZ, J. 1986. *More than the ABCs: The Early Stages of Reading and Writing*. Washington, DC: National Association for the Education of Young Children.

SCHICKEDANZ, J. 1990. *Adam's Righting Revolutions: One Child's Literacy Development from Infancy Through Grade One*. Portsmouth, NH: Heinemann.

SCHICKEDANZ, J. and CASBERGUE, R. 2004. *Writing in Preschool: Learning to Orchestrate Meaning and Marks*. Newark, DE: International Reading Association.

SCIESZKA, J. 1996. *The True Story of the Three Little Pigs*. New York: Scholastic.

SCHUELE, M. C., ROBERTS, D., FITZGERALD, F., and MOORE, M. 1993. "Assessing Emergent Literacy in Preschool Classrooms." *Day Care & Early Education 21*(2),13–21.

SIERRA, J. 1991. "Whole Language and Oral Tradition Literature or Pigs, Puppets, and Improv." *Emergency Librarian 19*(2), 14–17.

SIPE, L. R. 2002. "Talking Back and Taking Over: Young Children's Expressive Engagement During Storybook Read-Alouds." *The Reading Teacher 55*(5), 476–83.

SOLLEY, B. A. 2005. *When Poverty's Children Write: Celebrating Strengths, Transforming Lives*. Portsmouth, NH: Heinemann.

SOUNDY, C. S. 1993. "Let the Story Begin! Open the Box and Set Out Props." *Childhood Education 69*(3), 146–49.

SOUNDY, C. S. and GALLAGHER, P. W. 1993. "The Effects of Props on Young Children's Language Output During Story Retelling." *Ohio Reading Teacher 27*(2), 12–16.

STAUFFER, R. G. 1970. *The Language Experience Approach to the Teaching of Reading*. Newark, NJ: Harper Row.

STRICKLAND, D. S. and MORROW, L. M. 1989. "Environments Rich in Print Promote Literacy Behavior During Play." *Reading Teacher 43*(4), 330–31.

SULZBY, E. 1985. "Kindergartners as Readers and Writers." In M. Farr, ed., *Advances in Writing Research: Vol. 1, Children's Early Writing Development* (pp. 127–99). Norwood, NJ: Ablex.

SULZBY, E. 1986. "Writing and Reading: Signs of Oral and Written Language Organization in the Young Child." In W. Teale and E. Sulzby, eds., *Emergent Literacy: Writing and Reading* (pp. 51–89). Norwood, NJ: Ablex.

SULZBY, E. 1992. "Research Directions: Transitions from Emergent to Conventional Writing." *Language Arts 69*, 290–97.

SULZBY, E., BARNHART, J., and HEISHIMA, J. 1989. "Forms of Writing and Rereading from Writing: A Preliminary Report." In Mason, J., ed., *Reading/Writing Connections*. Boston: Allyn & Bacon.

SUNFLOWER, C. 1999. *75 Creative Ways to Publish Student Writing*. New York: Scholastic.

SUTTERBY, J. 2005. Scaffolding Play for English Language Learners. *Dimensions 33*(1), 24–29.

TAYLOR, N. E., BLUM, I. H., and LOGSDON, D. M. 1986. "The Development of Written Language Awareness: Environmental Aspects and Program Characteristics." *Reading Research Quarterly 21*, 131–49.

TEALE, W. H. and SULZBY, E. 1986. *Emergent Literacy: Writing and Reading*. Norwood, NJ: Ablex.

TEMPLE, C., NATHAN, R., TEMPLE, F., and BURRIS, N. 1993. *The Beginnings of Writing*. Third Edition. Boston: Allyn & Bacon.

TOMPKINS, G. E. 2004. *Teaching Writing: Balancing Process and Product*. Upper Saddle River, NJ: Pearson.

TOMPKINS, G. E. 2005. *Language Arts: Patterns of Practice*. Upper Saddle River, NJ: Pearson.

TRELEASE, J. 2006. *The Read Aloud Handbook*. Sixth Edition. New York: Penguin.

VEATCH, J., SAWICKI, F., ELLIOT, G., BARNETT, E., and BLACKEY, J. 1973. *Key Words to Reading: The Language Experience Approach Begins*. Columbus, OH: Merrill.

VUKELICH, C. 1990. "Where's the Paper? Literacy During Dramatic Play." *Childhood Education 67*, 205–209.

VUKELICH, C. 1994. "Effects of Play Interventions on Young Children's Reading of Environmental Print." *Early Childhood Research Quarterly 9*, 153–70.

VUKELICH, C. and VALENTINE, C. 1990. "A Child Plays: Two Teachers Learn." *Reading Teacher 44*(4), 342–44.

VYGOTSKY, L. S. 1962, 1986. *Thought and Language*. Cambridge, MA: MIT Press.

VYGOTSKY, L. S. 1966, 1967. "Play and Its Role in the Mental Development of the Child." *Soviet Psychology 12*, 67–76.

WARING-CHAFFEE, M. 1994. "'RDRNT...HRIKM' ('Ready or Not, Here I Come!'): Investigations in Children's Emergence as Readers and Writers." *Young Children 49*(6), 52–55.

WELLHOUSEN, K. and CROWTHER, I. 2004. *Creating Effective Learning Environments*. Florence, KY: Thomas Delmar Learning.

WONG FILLMORE, L. 1991. "When Learning a Second Language Means Losing the First." *Early Childhood Research Quarterly 6*, 323–46.

WOOD, M. 1999. *Essentials of Elementary Language Arts*. Second Edition. Needham Heights, MA: Allyn & Bacon.

YOLEN, J. and SCHOENHERR, J. 1987. *Owl Moon*. New York: Penguin Young Readers Group.